A History of HARRODSBURG

A History of
HARRODSBURG

Saratoga of the South

BOBBI DAWN RIGHTMYER

Published by The History Press
Charleston, SC
www.historypress.com

Cover images: A historical postcard of the last spring from Graham Springs, located on Linden Avenue in Young's Park, Harrodsburg; a historical postcard of Dr. Graham's Old Saloon Spring, located at Graham Springs.

First published 2022

Manufactured in the United States

ISBN 9781467149068

Library of Congress Control Number: 2021949212

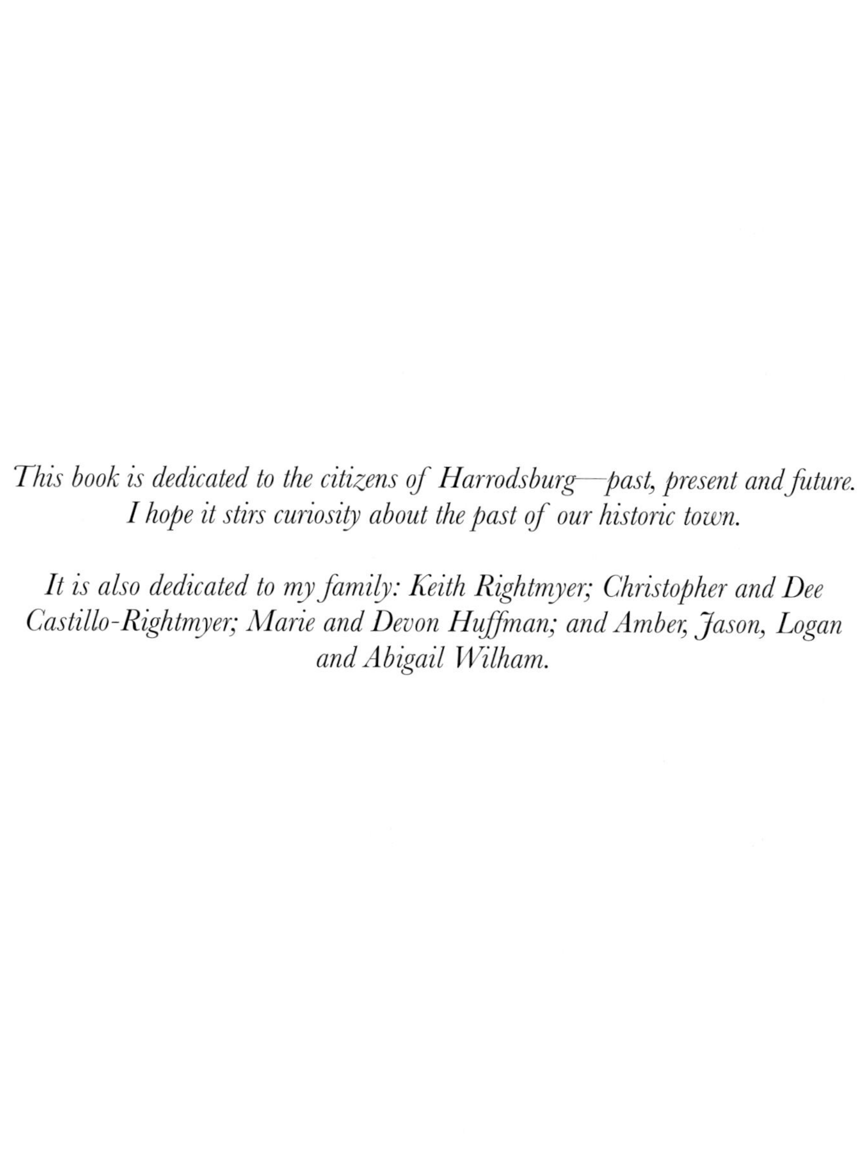

This book is dedicated to the citizens of Harrodsburg—past, present and future. I hope it stirs curiosity about the past of our historic town.

It is also dedicated to my family: Keith Rightmyer; Christopher and Dee Castillo-Rightmyer; Marie and Devon Huffman; and Amber, Jason, Logan and Abigail Wilham.

CONTENTS

ACKNOWLEDGEMENTS

As a writer of narrative nonfiction history, I have relied on research libraries and newspapers archives, as well as county records and personal recollections from Harrodsburg natives, to collect the information for this book. A long journey begins with just one step, and the journey of this book staggered into a great number of fine folks who offered knowledge and expertise. I can't thank them all personally, but I will name as many as possible. My sincerest apologies to any I missed.

First and foremost, I want to thank my husband, Keith Rightmyer, for his support, encouragement and photography skills, without which this book would not have been possible.

Secondly, I want to thank the following institutions and their employees for their assistance and inspiration: Harrodsburg Historical Society, Kentucky Historical Society, Filson Historical Society, Boyle County Historical Society, Capital City Museum, James Harrod Trust, Mercer County Chamber of Commerce, Harrodsburg First, Harrodsburg/Mercer County Tourism Commission, Armstrong Archives, Joseph's Dream, Farmstead at Shawnee Springs, Springfield Historical Society, James B. Haggin Memorial Hospital, Mercer County Public Library, Boyle County Public Library, Harvey Helm Memorial Library, Centre College Grace Doherty Library, Mercer County Deed Records, Beaumont Inn, Shaker Village of Pleasant Hill, University of Louisville, University of Kentucky, Transylvania University, *Harrodsburg Herald*, *Kentucky Democrat*, *Advocate-Messenger*, *Lexington Herald-Leader*, *Courier-Journal*, *Draper Manuscripts*, *Argus of Western America* and the History Press publishing team.

I also want to thank several local citizens for their encouragement and resources: Jerry L. Sampson, Stuart Sanders, Helen Dedman, Jill Cutler, Kandie Adkinson, Amalie Preston, Kay Keightley Foster, Marian Bauer, Kelly Scott Reed, Susan Thompson Barrington, Mary Cecil Thompson, Lisa Botner Goodrich, JoEtta Y. Wickliffe, Marsha Noel, Sarah Woods Bottom, Elizabeth Blair Bottom, Nancy Hill, Anna Armstrong, Mel Stewart Hankla and Michael Wisner.

A special thank-you to Larry Neuzel for scanning and formatting the photographs for this book. Without his help, there would be no photographs for readers to view.

Lastly, I could not have completed this book without the efforts of History Press commissioning editor Chad Rhoad. Even when the COVID pandemic shut down the country during 2020, Chad kept me plugging away. Thank you.

TIMELINE FOR THE SPRINGS OF HARRODSBURG

1769 Daniel Boone spends the winter of 1769–70 in a cave at Shawnee Springs.

1774 **June 16**. The Big Spring.

June. Fountainbleu Spring at Harrodsburg is founded. The first corn crops in Kentucky are planted near the Big Spring and at Fountainbleu Spring.

1775 **Fall and summer of 1776**. Old Fort Harrod is built on a hill above the Big Spring.

Summer. James Harrod builds on the out-lot at Boiling Spring. Boiling Spring Station becomes part of the Transylvania delegation with four representatives. Hugh McGary Station is founded at Shawnee Springs.

1776 **Summer**. William Pogue (wife of Ann McGinty) raises corn at Cove Spring.

1777 **June 22**. Barney Stagner is beheaded near the Fort Harrod Spring.

September 22. Corncrib skirmish at Cove Spring.

1779 **Spring**. Harrod fortifies Boiling Spring Station and builds the first large twin-chimney frame house in Kentucky.

1781 Ann McGinty founds and operates a fulling mill at Fort Harrod Spring.

1786 **April**. Harrod opens a Latin school at Boiling Spring Station.

1787 **November**. Harrod's stepson, James McDaniel, is killed at Boiling Spring; the Boiling Spring Latin School closes.

1788 Shawnee Springs house is built.

1801 Shawnee Springs house burns to the ground.

1805 George Thompson House is built at Shawnee Springs.

1806 Reverend Head discovers the healing powers of Greenville Springs.

1809 A new building is constructed at Greenville Springs.

1814 Greenville Springs comprises a total of 220 acres.

1816 Andrew Gore purchases Fort Harrod Spring from the Pogue heirs, and it becomes known as Gore Spring.

1817 Boise House is built at Fountainbleu.

1819 Sutton's Harrodsburg Springs is in operation when Dr. Christopher C. Graham moves to Harrodsburg.

1820 Sutton and Graham combine Sutton Springs and another small spring to make Harrodsburg Springs.

1825 **May 16**. Marquis de Lafayette visits Shawnee Springs during his national tour.

1826 **November 23**. Harrodsburg Springs purchases the Greenville Springs at auction.

1830 **May**. Graham deeds the Greenville Springs' buildings and twenty-four acres of land to Reverend William James; the Greenville Female Seminary would be run by Reverend James for three years.

May 9. General James Ray of Shawnee Springs dies.

1834 **May**. Greenville is sold to James Harlan.

1841 **February**. Graham's three musical slaves escape from Graham Springs.

1842 **Fall through spring 1843**. Graham Springs builds a huge new hotel and ballroom.

1845 **May**. Greenville Institute for Young Ladies is opened for students.

1849 **March**. Greenville is sold to Samuel Mullins.

1850 **July**. Graham Springs is expanded to 280 acres.

1851 **May 19**. Fire rages through the Greenville Institute for Young Ladies, and it burns to the ground.

1852 **June**. Nathaniel Parker Willis writes *Health Trips to the Tropics*, highlighting Graham Springs.

1853 **May 9**. Graham Springs is chosen as the location for the Western Military Asylum.

May 23. Graham sells the springs but keeps twenty-five acres for himself.

1854 **May**. Graham Springs becomes the United States Military Asylum.

1856 **August**. The government recommends the military asylum be discontinued.

September. New brick building at Greenville becomes Daughters College until 1893.

1859 **May 30**. Portions of the Graham Springs hotel burn to the ground.

1862 **October 8**. Graham Springs ballroom is used as a hospital during the Battle of Perryville.

1883 **May 5**. Fountainbleu Spring produces Kentucky Derby winner Leonatus.

1887 Jonathan I. Cassell buys the Graham Springs property and builds private residence.

1893 **June**. Daughters College is closed.

June. Greenville Springs College is run by Dr. J.M. Dalton and Miss Ovie Smedley for one school season.

1894 **September**. Greenville is bought by Colonel and Mrs. Thomas Smith and turned into Beaumont College.

1910 Plans are made to reestablish Graham Springs Resort on the Cassell property.

1911 **May**. Ben Allin turns the Cassell mansion into the new Graham Springs Hotel.

1912 Allin's Graham Springs Hotel is expanded.

1916 **May 6**. Fountainbleu Spring produces Kentucky Derby winner George Smith.

1917 **June**. Beaumont College is closed.

1920 Several new wells are drilled on Graham Springs property.

1924 **June 16**. 150th anniversary of Harrodsburg pageant is held at Graham Springs.

1929 **November 17**. Nancy Lewis Greene writes "Autumn at Graham Springs."

1932 **September 8**. Glave and Annie Bell Goddard buy Graham Springs.

1933 Graham Springs is opened as annex to Beaumont Inn.

1935 **May 2**. Mrs. Goddard sells Graham Springs to Mineral Springs Products Company Inc.

July. Mineral Springs becomes known as Graham Springs Sanitorium.

1937 Experiments begin at Graham Springs Sanitorium on concentrated colloidal sulfur.

1938 **July**. Dr. Ballard retires from Graham Springs Sanitorium.

1940 **June 20**. The Saloon Spring on the Graham Springs property is closed.

1945 **October**. Board of directors of A.D. Price Memorial Hospital buys Graham Springs Sanitorium.

1947 **April**. Funding is approved for the construction of Mercer General Hospital.

1954 **January 1**. Mercer General Hospital changes its name to James B. Haggin Memorial Hospital.

1961 Renfrew House restaurant is started at Shawnee Springs.

1974 George Thompson House at Shawnee Springs is listed in the National Register of Historic Places.

1982 **August 21**. George Thompson House is partially destroyed by fire.

2005 James B. Haggin Memorial Hospital is expanded.

2017 Ephraim McDowell Regional Medical Center buys James B. Haggin Memorial Hospital.

2019 The Farmstead at Shawnee Springs is opened.

INTRODUCTION

During the late pioneer period of Kentucky, as Native American warfare faded to a grim memory, towns began to expand and the economy strengthened. At last Kentuckians had the time and money, as well as a long-suppressed urge, for entertainment and relaxation. In an astonishingly short period, many humble salt licks, with their medicinal waters, were transformed into glittering, sophisticated and fashionable spas where the elite and well-to-do came from all over the country to take the waters and have a fabulous time doing it.

Staying healthy in early Kentucky was no easy thing. If the Native Americans, wild animals and hard work did not put an untimely end to the Kentucky pioneer, untreated illnesses were quick to do so. There were few doctors on the frontier, although considering the state of medical knowledge in the eighteenth and nineteenth centuries, this may not have been all bad.

Early Kentuckians did have a few medical advantages, and one of them was an abundance of mineral springs. The pioneers had long known and made use of medicinal or "healing" springs. Entire families would camp near such a spring so an afflicted member could drink the healing water or bathe in it or both. People thought they knew which springs helped which ailments, and they sought out the ones they needed for their unique problems.

As time passed, this practice became as customary for the wealthy as for the less affluent Kentuckians. The difference was that the wealthy took the waters in much more elaborate surroundings, patterned on the spas developers had known in the eastern states. These sanitoriums were built to imitate famous European spas.

In the early and mid-nineteenth century, every spa published analyses of its waters and competed with rivals for doctors' testimonials and recommendations. A cheerful atmosphere was also deemed an important factor in successful health recovery, lending rationale for the elaborate entertainments offered at the medicinal spas.

Taking the waters became popular for social as well as medical reasons, and attracting guests from far and wide became a competitive business. Not everyone who summered at a watering place was ill. Far from it. If one person in a family felt indisposed and the entire family could afford it, they would pack up—servants and all—and go to take the waters. If no one was ill, the springs were thought of as first-rate preventive medicine environment, particularly during cholera, yellow fever and other epidemics. But many people shamelessly went to spas to have a good time.

According to Coleman's "Old Kentucky Watering Places," in the heyday of the fashionable watering places, there were 125 resorts in Kentucky, and several had national reputations. Fine foods and beverages, dancing, gaming, walking, riding and hunting were standard at most of the popular spas, and Harrodsburg was no exception. Graham Springs had cotillion parties conducted by a "professor of dancing" along with its entertainments. Greenville Springs announced a "regular theatrical company of respectable performers" as well as "the best band of music that can be procured."

In the 1820s, Dr. Daniel Drake visited most of Kentucky's mineral springs. One of the more popular of these advertised the health-giving qualities of the water and the additional advantage "to mix and mingle with the best society in the State." Dr. Drake gave Graham Springs first place and noted the waters to be effective in cases of dyspepsia and in urinary problems. Board, lodging and medical attention was ten dollars per week, but the rate was reduced for those who remained at the spa longer.

Even transportation facilities were improved to make it easier for people to visit these health spas. Resorts were often in rural areas off the main roads, and smart resort owners made sure that all available carriages, stagecoaches, boats and, later, trains were used to keep arriving and departing guests as comfortable as possible.

Most of the watering places appealed to all members of the family. While they offered brilliant dancing balls and excellent "wining and dining," with plenty of opportunity for romance and matchmaking, they also provided such family diversions as croquet, horseshoes for the gentlemen, lawn tennis and other games all ages could enjoy. The personality of the resort host, his management practices and his imagination and skill in providing amenities and entertainment determined the atmosphere of the watering place and the type of guests who returned year after year.

Some of Kentucky's watering places boasted several different types of springs. In Coleman's "Old Watering Places," the most common were "salt, salt-sulphur, white sulphur, black sulphur, red sulphur, chalybeate (iron), vitriol, alum, copperas, and Epsom springs, the use of which could be diuretic and cathartic in effect." This variety was important and well publicized because it meant spas with more than one type of spring could attract guests in need of various treatments and keep them for the season, rather than have them move on to rival establishments.

Attracting patrons became a highly competitive affair, with each resort issuing promotional tracts and running newspaper advertisements. These advertisements included appreciative testimonials written by the formerly sick and now miraculously restored customers, as well as descriptions of newly added amenities, facilities and entertainments and chemical analyses of the waters by medical authorities, who often compared the waters to celebrated European spas. For instance, in Van Arsdall's *A Medical History of the Harrodsburg Springs*, Dr. Daniel Drake stated that "the waters of Harrodsburg and Graham Springs measured up to Seidlitz Springs in Bohemia, the former Czech Republic." Graham Springs was also compared to Baden-Baden Springs in Germany.

Although there was much controversy at the Greenville Springs because it went through many different owners, the "watering seasons" of 1806–10 were the height of occupancy for the resort. Greenville Springs announced a "regular theatrical company of respectable performers," as well as "the best band of music that can be procured." According to Fortescue Cumings, the noted English traveler, it was a "gay place more given to cards, billiards, horse jockeying, &, than to the use of waters for medicinal purposes."[1]

Sutton's Harrodsburg Springs was owned by Captain David Sutton in the early 1820s. His son-in-law, Dr. Christopher Columbus Graham, built a four-story hotel, allowing the spa to accommodate one thousand patrons. In the 1830s and '40s, the prime peak of the spa, visitors came from all parts of the United States as well as foreign countries. The personality of Dr. Graham, his management practices and his imagination and skill provided amenities and entertainment, which seasoned the atmosphere of the watering place and the type of guests who returned year after year.

A *Courier-Journal* article from 1942 talks about the many "watering places" located in Kentucky and used before the advent of the Civil War. It is said that physicians strongly recommended taking the waters, which were advertised as being "especially beneficial to persons suffering from diseases of the stomach, liver and kidneys, as well as from asthma, gout, dyspepsia, rheumatism, bilious disorders, neuralgia, autumnal fevers and general debility." It is said that "there was much flirting, sometimes by 'married charmers, thirsting for universal dominion.' Disputes between the ladies often involved 'pillows, bolsters, fingernails and the poignant sarcasm of the tongue,' and, at time, the dueling pistols of sensitive gentlemen could be heard in a nearby woodland settling 'affairs of honor.'"

While researching *A History of Harrodsburg: Saratoga of the South*, it was noted that several important names have different spellings throughout historical documents. The names VanArsdall and Fountainbleu are very prominent; however, there are several different spellings: Vanarsdal, VanArsdal, Van Arsdall, Fountain Bleu, Fountain Blue and Fountainbleu. For continuity throughout this book, I will use the modern spelling of each name, VanArsdall and Fountainbleu, unless used in a direct quote.

Chapter 1

THE GREENVILLE SPRINGS

1806–1900

Greenville Springs, the nucleus of which was a group of log cabins in which invalids who desired the benefit of the water, lived, bringing their own furniture and supplies of food, in the last of the 18th century.
—Maria Thompson Daviess, History of Mercer and Boyle Counties, 1924

"Best Mineral Water in Any State Bordering the Ohio River"

Greenville Springs was a well-known resort in Harrodsburg, Kentucky, in the early nineteenth century. Reverend Jesse Head, the itinerant Methodist minister who married Abraham Lincoln's parents, discovered the springs on the farm of Lucas VanArsdall in 1806. According to the article "The Springs at Harrodsburg" by Mai Flournoy Van Deren Van Arsdall in *The Register of the Kentucky Historical Society*, Reverend Head, after spending a few days in Harrodsburg with Rebecca Hart and other Methodist friends in the summer of 1806, was "suffering from poor health." He soon discovered the "beneficial qualities" of the water from a mineral spring on VanArsdall's property and became enthusiastic about the curative powers of the iron and saline water. He returned to Springfield and declared that this was "the best mineral water in any state bordering on the Ohio River."

A historical postcard of the cabin where Abraham Lincoln's parents were married. The cabin is now inside a brick temple at Old Fort Harrod State Park. *Author's collection.*

On Reverend Head's advice, Felix Grundy, a judge from Springfield, bought half interest in the property in the summer of 1806 and, along with VanArsdall, began building a travelers' lodge. Judge Grundy put up $1,900 in bonds and cash to purchase a moiety, or one-half interest, in the "228-acre plantation of Arsdall adjoining the town lands of Harrodsburg on the south containing the mineral or medicinal springs." Mercer County Circuit Court Records show that the purchase agreement was not well drafted. The last paragraph was written in a different style and, almost as an afterthought, appears to require Grundy to pay an additional $500 to VanArsdall "so soon as a bond given by William Duval to Grundy becomes due which is sometime in the next year."[2]

Accommodations for visitors were needed in a hurry because of a "great collection of people at the Springs" was predicted during the summer. The purchase price was used by the partners to begin a frenzied building program. Henry Speed, a banker from Danville, was interested enough to offer to purchase one-half interest. Even though his offer was not accepted, he was a frequent visitor at the springs and made this statement:

> *I believe the virtues of the water were discovered in the latter part of the summer or early in the fall of 1806. No considerable resort was had to*

The Rebecca Hart Cabin in Harrodsburg, Kentucky, circa 1940s. This photo shows the chimney side with sign before it was razed. *Library of Congress.*

The Rebecca Hart Cabin was the site of the first Methodist prayer meetings held in Harrodsburg in the early 1800s. *Library of Congress.*

> *the "springplace" shortly before Grundy purchased, nor were there any improvements of value made in consequence of such discovery until Grundy purchased. A large, framed house and a number of cabins were built at the "Springs" after the purchase of Grundy…some post and railing were done and there was a GREAT collection of people at the "Springs"…in 1807 and 1808.*[3]

Although there is no definitive proof how Greenville Springs got its name, there are a few possibilities. During this time in Harrodsburg history, members of the prominent Green family lived in this vicinity. Also, there is mention of a little settlement called Greenville near this place, but this information has not been substantiated. It is this author's opinion that both the Greenville Springs and Greenville Street in Harrodsburg were named to commemorate the 1795 Treaty of Greenville with the Northwestern Indians. This treaty, formally titled Treaty with the Wyandots, in effect until 1812, was important and meaningful to Kentuckians. The treaty redefined the boundary between Native America territory and lands available for American settlement.[4]

People were soon visiting family and friends in Harrodsburg to try this "spring" water for themselves, but there were no public accommodations

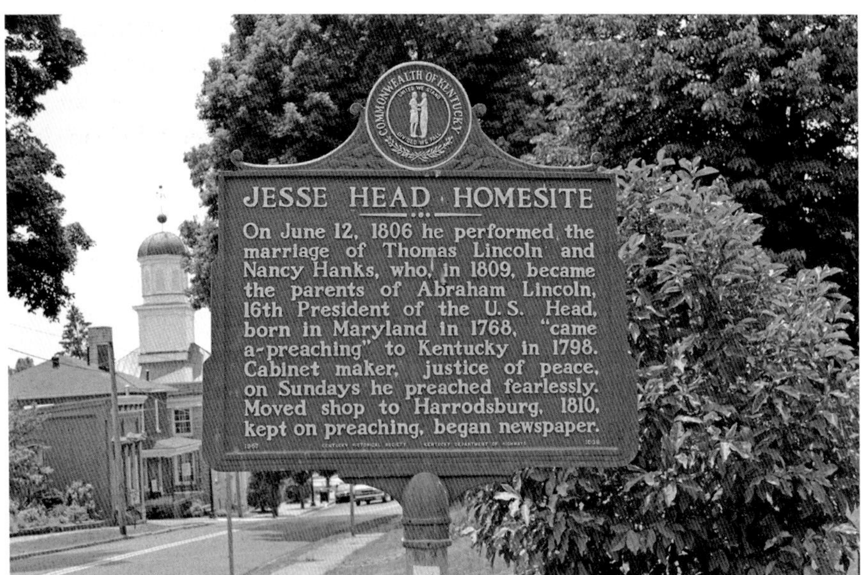

The historical marker for Reverend Jesse Head, located in Springfield, Kentucky. *Keith Rightmyer.*

of any size. Judge Grundy, realizing what an incredible business venture this would be, worked with VanArsdall to build cabins and stables.

Friends, relatives and local workmen all helped during the fall of 1806 and during the next spring and summer. Contracts were signed for many new buildings, and extensive repairs were made to the "old house and old stable" by Samuel Hodges. Hay was cut, fencing put up and a large garden planted in the spring of 1807. William Mann, John McCool, James Westerfield and a Mr. Negley built about twenty-one new cottages, and George Slaughter's son was paid for "daubing" (covering) them. Garret Cozine and Abraham VanArsdall built a "60 by 40-foot-long log-cabin dining room," a new springhouse and a big new kitchen. By far the most expensive and pretentious building they constructed was a large new "framed" house that cost between $700 and $900. Considering the new kitchen cost $20 and the new springhouse $18, this large new house must have offered spacious quarters for a great many guests. Chimneys were raised and topped; nails, padlocks, hasps, hinges, staples, locks and keys were bought; and the accounts were kept by a Mr. Weatherford, who soon proved to be an unsatisfactory clerk and bookkeeper.[5]

With so much activity going on, the partners knew that they needed someone to set up and run the tavern and to serve as proprietor of the new Greenville Springs. Grundy and VanArsdall made a trip to Springfield and, with Reverend Head accompanying them, went to the tavern of Daniel Jennings to persuade him that he was the man for this job. Jennings said, "Grundy and Van Arsdall were very anxious for me to occupy the Springs and held out to me that they would continue immediately with the improvements." Reverend Head drew up the following interesting and wordy agreement:

> *This ____ day of June, 1807, this article of agreement entered into by Lucas Van Arsdal and Felix Grundy and Daniel Jennings…witnesseth… that the said partnership of Van Arsdal & Grundy hath let to the said Jennings, for the Term of Five years from this date, the plantation on which the said VanArsdall now lives in Mercer County with the buildings thereunto belonging for the purpose of keeping a Public House for the accommodation of those, as well as others, who may attend the Medical Springs on said place.*
>
> *The said Jennings, on his part, is to furnish and appropriate all the Household and Kitchen furniture now in his possession for the aforesaid purpose, also two Negro Men and a Negro Girl; also two or three Milch Cows. An inventory of the said Furniture shall be made out, and the same*

> *returned to the said endings, at the expiration of said Term, and the said Van Arsdal and Grundy are to pay for two-thirds of all the House hold furniture necessary to be purchased by the said Jennings for the use of the premises during the Term aforesaid, also pay their equal part of the expense of Hiring Servants for the said premises, and at the expiration of said Term the Furniture so purchased shall be equally divided between the said Van Arsdal, Grundy and Jennings. An able Clerk who understands Book-keeping shall be procured who shall keep an accurate account of all the expenditures and profits arising from the said premises—Which profits shall be equally divided between the said Van Arsdal, Grundy, Jennings.... The Cabbins now built and hereinafter to be built, for the accommodations of Foreigners, shall be an equal expense to Grundy and Van Arsdal—as likewise the new dining room now building. The said Van Arsdal, Grundy, and Jennings to pay each one-third of the Hire of the said Clerk. It is to be understood that the said Jennings has the liberty of dissolving this contract at the end of any one year, provided he shall give three months' notice in writing, to the said Grundy and Van Arsdal.*[6]

Judge Grundy remained in Springfield for a few days to attend business and during this time sent a letter to Harrodsburg for Mr. Lucas VanArsdall:

> *Sir:*
>
> *...Mr. Jennings and myself have agreed for him to live on the place if you can give immediate possession and I really think it would be very much to the interest of us all.*
> *I am yrs*
>
> *F. Grundy*[7]

VanArsdall moved to property he owned "three or four miles distant" but spent his time overseeing the building at the "Springs." Daniel Jennings brought his wife, family servants and furniture from Springfield to Greenville Springs and paid Samuel Robinson eight pounds, five shillings for moving his possessions and the "tavern tables" to Harrodsburg.

According to the *Kentucky Gazette* (August 1812), Mrs. Grundy, Miss Gilky and Eliza Jones were paid for sewing curtains, coverlets and "bed-clothes," and purchases were made of thread, needles, pins, beeswax, thimbles, knitting needles, wool, linen, flax, linsey, cotton and muslin. The new buildings were being completed while Jennings rode over to Bardstown and Danville to hire extra servants. In Frankfort, he hired "Phillis" to cook for the new tavern at the "Springs" for forty dollars per annum. However, busy as Jennings must have been, he attended horse races in all three places, and the account books record the fact that he lost money at all three events. Mr. Berry, the new clerk and bookkeeper, began keeping the accounts, making his entries in pounds, shillings and pence.

A news snippet, also found in the *Kentucky Gazette*, showed that Jennings was conscious of his new position and responsibility, so he bought himself a new straw hat, paid the tailor for "cutting and sewing a new coat," had a "hair trimming" and even bought a toothbrush. Ten pairs of slippers, several pairs of shoes and shoe leather for Phill, Dan and Dinor—his servants—were purchased from "Speed the shoemaker." Mrs. Jennings also got a new bonnet (the "English Gypsey Bonnet, The Superior Village Hat, and the Mistic Bonnet" were most fashionable millinery of the time), new shoes, a "band and shift" and extra money for other necessities.[8]

The most important item bought, for a payment of three pounds to the Commonwealth of Kentucky, was a tavern license. The license was necessary to purchase meat and foodstuff for the dining room, grain and feed for the stables and liquor for the tavern. Melons were bought from local people; beef from Mr. Comingo; pork from Mr. Cozine, Mr. Grady and Mr. C. VanArsdall; corn from Mr. MaGoffin; grain from Mr. Gaines and Mr. Akins; and bacon from Mr. A. Slaughter and Mr. Robert McAfee. Sugar, meal, flour, salt, tea, butter, tobacco, camphor, alum, tallow, cider, brandy, Sangaree (wine) and even "100 Segars" (cigars) all were purchased as locally as possible. Many names appear in the early account books such as John L. Bridges, who was paid for "bringing papers from Natchez," and Henry Smock, who "helped with the horses."

The success of the new Greenville Springs was soon heard all over the state, and hundreds of people congregated there during the "watering season," which lasted from late May until mid-September, with the largest number of people there in July and August 1807. So many people arrived that beds and bedclothes had to be rented from many of Harrodsburg's families. The Armstrongs, McAfees, McKamys, Mithells, Moores, Cookes, Thompsons and Johnsons were paid for "rent on beds and loss of bed-cloathes." Some furniture was bought at Hough's (Huff) Sale, and Reverend Head was paid later for making several pieces in his cabinet shop. Everyone was so busy that Head, a very frequent visitor, had to help keep the books that summer.

One sad note is recorded for this busy season. Colonel John Logan, treasurer of Kentucky and a brother of General Benjamin Logan, founder of Logan's Station, attempted to restore his feeble health at Greenville Springs. Unfortunately, he died and was buried at Harrodsburg on July 16, 1807, in the "graveyard just south of the old fort with only a plain stone to mark the spot."[9]

Fight for Billiard Table at Greenville Springs

Daniel Jennings, on December 20, 1807, bought Grundy's share in Greenville Springs. The Mercer County Deed Book lists the sale of this property for $2,500 for the undivided half interest in a tract of 227 acres adjoining Harrodsburg, "being the tract on which the Greenville Springs are situated." Grundy decided, because of his new legal appointment, to move to Tennessee and therefore sold his interest in the Greenville Springs. He was still vitally interested in the springs because he let Jennings and VanArsdall have bonds and cash to continue paying the workmen for the improvements that were being made; he also wrote several letters from Tennessee attempting to straighten out some of their business arrangements.

A new agreement was drawn up between the two remaining partners:

> *Van Arsdal and Jennings agree as follows: Jennings pays two-thirds all expenses and labor at the place he now lives and draws two-thirds of the profits. Van Arsdal pays one-third and draws one-third of profits—and every expense except as herein excepted, is included. The services of Mr. and Mrs. Jennings to be thrown in. The improvements made on the place to be equally borne by each. If Jennings Chooses to Get a Billiard Table, He Does It at His Own Expense and He Has the Profits. This contract continues for four years from the twenty-fourth of June next…given under our hands and seals this 21st December 1807.*
>
> *Test: F. Grundy and John Fleece, Junior.*
> *D. Jennings and Lucas Van Arsdal*[10]

Jennings made several improvements and changes that did not meet with the approval of VanArsdall. Windows were put into the new "barr-room," and the bone of contention, a billiard table, was purchased for "45 pounds, one shilling, and a half penny." Hal Speed "attended" the billiard table, and the license for operating it cost five dollars.[11]

Newspaper advertising was effective during this time. The Frankfort paper, the *Western World*, announced on April 8, 1808, that after June 1, Jennings would be able "to accommodate any number of boarders who may choose to call on him" and further stated that "the water is free to all that may board on the premises or rent cabbins." During this season, more than 1,500 people came to Greenville Springs, including "some of the most efficient physicians of the Western Country, and attested to the efficacy of the waters." In Jennings's words, "We had a GREAT MANY boarders in the summer of 1808, and the partnership took in 734 pounds, fourteen shillings eleven pence and 500 pounds in bonds."[12]

With this successful season ending, everyone should have been satisfied, but profits were consumed by the many bills to be paid, "[a]lmost if not entirely the whole of the profits has been absorbed by the large expenditures requisite in the commencement and the early stages of this business in improvements on the premises and in articles of furniture and other necessaries in the preparation of the House for the reception of the visitants to the Springs," as Jennings described it.

VanArsdall, the straitlaced Dutch Reform member of the partnership, did not approve of the billiard table, the barroom and the worldly ways of Jennings and some of the guests. When John Jouitt of Versailles, Henry Speed of Danville and Thomas Eastland of Woodford County each showed an interest in purchasing one-half of Greenville Springs, VanArsdall decided to sell.

Recently appointed a trustee for Woodford Academy, Eastland and his wife, Nancy, visited Greenville Springs on the way to Elk River in Tennessee. In W.T. Smith's *A Complete Index to…Littell's Laws of Kentucky*, the Eastlands returned for a stay of two weeks, and during this time, Eastland talked with VanArsdall "near the [plum] orchard" about purchasing the property. So enthusiastic was the prospective purchaser that he told his friend, Robert Moseley of Green County, "When I buy the 'Springs' the profits there will more than pay for my trip to Elk River." Eastland invited VanArsdall to Versailles to discuss the sale, and when Jennings "understood my partner had gone over the Kentucky River to see about selling his interest in the 'Springs,' I sen[t] word by VanArsdall's little son, Luke, not to be in too great a hurry to sell."[13]

An account of the meeting in Versailles is given by Samuel Brooking of Woodford County:

In the late summer of 1808 I was at the house of Captain Thomas Eastland and understood he hourly expected a Captain Van Arsdal at his house to close a contract or make one with him relative to Eastland purchasing the "Springs" near Harrodsburg and Van Arsdal not coming as soon as he expected, Eastland said he would not for $1000 fail to make the purchase. After a few hours, just as Eastland and I were on our horses to start to Versailles, Van Arsdal came, and Eastland returned to the house with him.[14]

VanArsdall sold the Greenville Springs property and signed both a bond and a bill of sale. These two "legal papers" were in Eastland's handwriting and signed before witnesses who were his friends. VanArsdall requested copies of the documents but did not receive them; as a result of this business transaction, there arose far-reaching complications, lawsuits, name-calling and finally a decision by the Court of Appeals of Kentucky. Because of the constant reference to these documents in the records of Greenville Springs, they are included here:

The Bond: For value received of Thomas Eastland, I bind myself…to convey to him…one equal and undivided half of the Greenville Springs tract of land containing two hundred and twenty eight acres of land…it is expressly understood that said Eastland is to be put into immediate possession of the full enjoyment of one Equal and undivided half of the before mentioned tract of land together with one full half of all the Buildings and improvements of every kind as also of the Medical Springs and other natural advantages whatever, which possession, however, is not to do away [with] *my former contracts as to Grundy and Jennings…5th day August, 1808.*

The Bill of Sale [later referred to as the "written contract"]:

I, Lucas Van Arsdal,…granted bargained and sold unto Thomas Eastland…all the property which I possess at the Greenville Springs in said Mercer County, which is now in the possession of Daniel Jennings at the said Springs. Consisting of one yoke of work steers, one wagon, seven head of cows, hogs, sheep &; the crop of corn now growing, oats of the present crop, as also the hay that was cut this season, together with all and Every other kind of crop, including the garden, orchard, one mare, one coalt, and one horse &…and the farming utensials of Every kind. The Household and Kitchen furniture…table furniture…beads and bead furniture of every kind and description…provisions, Liquors, Stable forage &&…I am also

Greenville Springs,
(Harrodsburgh, Kentucky.)

THE Subscribers having taken possession of the Greenville Springs, as proprietors, inform the public that the house will be continued as when under the superintendance of John Hanna, for the accommodation of all those who may think proper to call. The arrangements that are now making, in addition to the present improvements, will enable them to render comfortable and agreeable, those who may resort to the Springs.

AMOS EDWARDS,
DANIEL M. HEARD,

Nov. 25th, 1820.—50tf

Above: A historical sketch of the original Greenville Springs. *Beaumont Inn Collection.*

Left: A newspaper clipping for the Greenville Springs from the *Kentucky Gazette*, August 9, 1821. *Author's collection.*

entitled to one-third part of all money which may be or has bin-received by said Jennings on account of the tavern, the rent of Cabbins &&…I do hereby tranfurr to said Eastland and do hereby full Inpower him to settle the account with the said Jennings…

Lucas Van Arsdal

I give up to Mr. Van Arsdal the higher wheels of the wagon and axeltrue.

Thomas Eastland[15]

Van Arsdall's "The Springs at Harrodsburg" states that Eastland's verbal agreement was to pay £1,000 for the property in the follow manner: 1) one hundred acres of land in Woodford County to be transferred to VanArsdall,

$1,200; 2) a note held by Eastland on Richard Young, $500; 3) "Ausbin," a Black man, $500; 4) a Black woman and her child, $550; 5) a note from Eastland, due in two years, $200; and 6) a note held by Eastland to John Whitaker for £116 and 5 shillings.

Eastland came to Harrodsburg immediately, brought workmen to erect a 112-foot-long wooden portico on the large "framed" house and took over the management of Greenville Springs early in 1809. By May 16, Eastland was in full charge and announced in the *Kentucky Gazette* the erection of several new buildings and the addition of stable space sufficient to accommodate the animals of one hundred more guests. Visitors were assured that his "ballroom was elegantly furnished" and that "no exceptions will be made wanting to accommodate them to their entire satisfaction." The best bands of music were engaged to attend during the watering season, for the amusement of dancing parties.[16]

This change in partnership did not please Jennings, and even though Eastland offered to purchase his one-half interest, Jennings chose to sell to Montgomery Bell of Dickson County, Tennessee. Bell, a wealthy merchant, was well known in Lexington and Nicholasville and obviously had been a visitor at Greenville Springs.[17]

No one had been of greater help to the original partners (and no one enjoyed the mineral waters more) than Reverend Jesse Head. VanArsdall and Jennings must have discussed his many helpful acts because they deeded Head a one-acre lot bordering on the town limits and near the medicinal springs for the low price of ten dollars. He was to have "free and uninterrupted use of the Medical Water on the land of VanArsdal…for the Reverend Jesse Head, his family, and heirs…but the above interest shall not extend to any Boarders he may keep at any time on the said premises." They appreciated what he had done, but they were not going to allow any competition.[18]

The grave of Reverend Jesse Head (1768–1842), located at Springhill Cemetery, Harrodsburg. *Keith Rightmyer.*

Business affairs had been so hectic and confused that no actual deeds had been recorded by Grundy or Jennings. Therefore, on August 22, 1809, Lucas VanArsdall and his wife, Jenny, deeded to Montgomery Bell for $2,500 "a one-half interest in 227 acres, excepting the one-

In Kentucky Hemp Fields. STANDING, SPREAD AND SHOCKED.

This page: Historical postcards of a Mercer County hemp field, circa 1910. *Author's collection.*

acre lot deeded to Reverend Head, being the tract on which the Greenville Springs are situated." This was the portion passed from VanArsdall to Grundy to Jennings, while the other half had just been sold by VanArsdall to Eastland. Greenville Springs and its new owners, now past the hectic period of preparing for the public, were ready to settle down and enjoy the growing widespread popularity of the newly famous spa.[19]

Eastland was living at the Greenville Springs and acting as host and proprietor, while Daniel and Sarah Jennings continued running the tavern;

visitors were enjoying "mixing and mingling with the best society of the State." However, under the surface, all was not going smoothly. Eastland needed ready cash to continue building and quietly mortgaged his interest in the property to Montgomery Bell. A deed was actually recorded, even though Eastland had no intention of giving up as proprietor. For a quick year-round, moneymaking scheme, Bell and Eastland decided to establish a "ropewalk," a hemp rope factory, on twelve of the seventy-five acres of the property across the Harrodsburg-Danville road from the entrance to Greenville Springs. This factory quickly brought in the needed cash; more buildings were erected, lavish parties and balls were given and visitors came in increasing numbers to enjoy this expanding and fashionable summer resort.[20]

The Fight for Greenville Springs

The successful surface view of Greenville Springs was deceiving because in 1811, a full-fledged, hostile, name-calling argument was taken to the Circuit Court of Mercer County. Few cases in the records show as much bitterness as this one. VanArsdall refused to give a deed to the Greenville Springs tract of land because Eastland did not even own the Woodford County land promised in exchange for the transfer. The slaves he promised had long since bought their freedom, and the "Bill of Sale" under which Eastland was claiming the property was "counterfeit and forged" and not the actual one VanArsdall had signed. Eastland, in turn, claimed compensation of $1,950 because VanArsdall had verbally included the billiard table, some rented furniture, a mare and larger profits from the tavern than actually existed. Samuel Davis and James Haggin, prominent Harrodsburg lawyers, represented VanArsdall. Isham Talbot, from Versailles, was Eastland's lawyer.

Claims and counterclaims were aired in court, and prominent area men gave depositions: Thomas Allen and his son John (Mercer County clerk and deputy), Captain Abraham Chaplin, William Allen, John Thompson, James Harlan, John Haggin and his son John (Mercer County sheriff and deputy), Major Burton, Henry Higgins, John Williams, Samuel Brooking, Isaac Mitchell, Henry Palmer, Captain William Bohannon, Robert Atwood, Garret Cozine, Cornelius Darnaby, Carret Dorland, Robert Perry, Robert Mosely, Henry Speed, Captain Nathaniel Hart and James Campbell. Judge Grundy and J.M. Lewis sent depositions from Tennessee.

Speed said, "Eastland represented to me that there was a difference in the Written Contract and the Bargain," and back in 1808, he felt that "a dispute would arise" because VanArsdall was not "acquainted with the contract as Eastland represent it." Hart said he had known VanArsdall "since 1788 or '89 and always considered him a careful and honest man, but one for whom making such a large contract might prove hard." Eastland he had known since 1796 and had often heard him spoken of as a "high finished sharper…a keen hard man in a bargain." Harlan deposed, "Eastland and I have lived as neighbors and Eastland is considered a 'sharper' in his dealings."

In the May term of Mercer Circuit Court, VanArsdall won the suit, and Eastland's part of the Greenville Springs property reverted to VanArsdall. Bell's recent deed from Eastland was not legal either, and he brought suit to recover "the four or five thousand dollars" he had invested in the new buildings. Nothing came of this suit because it was proved that "Bell had made much more than that from the 'ropewalk.'" Eastland did not give up easily, and even though he had been judged wrong by the court and the people who best knew the facts, on June 18, 1812, he entered an appeal to the Kentucky Court of Appeals. This case was not decided until April 12, 1814. Judge Logan wrote the opinion, which stated:

> *There is some gross and palpable error in this business and although not within the grasp or explanation of the chancellor, yet too obviously lurks, to receive the interposition of a Court of Equity for a specific enforcement. The case, to say the least of it, presents a contract which is unreasonably hard and unconscientious, and as such cannot be specifically enforced.… The decree, therefore, of the Circuit Court* [Mercer] *must be affirmed with costs.*[21]

Eastland Ejected from Greenville Springs

During the period in which the suit was pending, Eastland was legally "ejected" from Greenville Springs and moved with his family to Tennessee. Henry Palmer, former sheriff of Mercer County and a justice of the peace, took over as proprietor of the Greenville Springs and ran it successfully until 1819. Palmer owned no part of the property but made an excellent manager.

VanArsdall, the disillusioned and unwilling owner, was still anxious to sell his interest in the property. He found Thomas Deye Owings of Bath County, a wealthy citizen and iron manufacturer of Lexington and Owingsville, ready to purchase one-half of Greenville Springs purely as a business investment. Owings, soon after the War of 1812, had bought Olympian Springs in Bath County as an investment.[22]

Greenville Springs was increasing in value because when Owings received his deed on August 31, 1814, the purchase price was $7,000. Two one-acre lots, the one given Reverend Head and one VanArsdall kept for himself, were specifically accepted in this property transfer. In 1815, Reverend Head sold his lot near the springs to Mrs. Eleanor Kincaid when she moved from Lexington. His deed to her stipulated that she "could not keep boarders who might use the mineral water." Reverend Head sold this property in order to purchase "in-lot" 152 to establish his business, "Head and Winn—Cabinet Makers."[23]

The publicity that came from the lawsuit and the change in ownership did not hurt business at Greenville Springs in any way. Palmer advised the owners to build bathing houses where "baths warm and cold" were offered to the visitors. The "best bands of music engaged to attend" the nightly dances in the refurbished ballroom and a new gentlemen's bar of "extensive proportions" were advertised as new enticements in the *Kentucky Reporter* during 1814 and 1815.

General John Adair was at Greenville Springs on August 28, 1815, and found the surroundings so exhilarating that he wrote to his friend Colonel Anderson of the healthful aspects of the place and included his political views on current issues. Five years later, somewhat to his chagrin, this letter was printed in James Armstrong's paper, the *Olive Branch and Western Union*, while Adair was running for governor of Kentucky.[24]

Noah Miller Ludlow, a well-known actor and producer of the early nineteenth century, visited Greenville Springs in 1816, and his journal gives a description of the "extensiveness of the establishment" at that time:

> *They are a place of considerable resort during the hot summer months… the elite of Kentucky are the visitors of these springs, where most of the give themselves up to rural pleasures and social parties…dissipation and extravagance is not carried to any extent in this fashionable watering-place. The grounds at these Springs are covered by the main building on one side of the front lawn—with the line of cottages on the opposite side and at one end—leaving the other end open for a main entrance or approach from the road. Between these tenements is a grass lawn, pleasantly shaded by lofty trees. These cottages are generally taken by families for the summer.*[25]

So glowing were the accounts of Kentuckians and visitors from other states that two Harrodsburg businessmen, Harrison Munday and John Hanna, decided that absentee owners should not reap all the profits. They offered $20,000 for the property. August 24, 1818, was agreed on as the day for transfer of deeds. Bell, who had mortgaged his one-half interest to Perter Hoffman Jr. of Baltimore, paid off his mortgage and gave a clear title to the new owners, receiving $10,000. Owings gave their deed to Munday and Hanna and received $10,000. The value of Greenville Springs had risen rapidly over of period of just twelve years.[26]

A Time of Value and Popularity at Greenville Springs

This marked the high point in both value and popularity of Greenville Springs, for now a small, unpretentious rival, Harrodsburg Springs, opened its doors to visitors. Three years before, Captain David Sutton, a well-to-do hat manufacturer of Harrodsburg, had discovered another "Epsom" spring on one of several "out-lots" he owned in the southern section of the town limits. This mineral spring, even though it was inside the city limits, was less than a half mile from the main Greenville Spring. The properties of the new spring differed somewhat from the mineral water at the established spa, and because Harrodsburg was becoming known throughout the whole South as a health resort, everyone felt that Sutton was wise in opening Harrodsburg Springs to the public in 1818. Humble in the beginning, the smaller Harrodsburg Springs would become world renowned and completely overshadow and absorb Greenville Springs.[27]

Undaunted by any hints of a rival, Munday and Hanna added a "large and commodious dining ballroom and a theatre," built several new cottages and laid out a "Pleasure Garden" at Greenville Springs. Hanna took the lead in the business activities because he was considered a very promising and enterprising young man. At the time of his marriage to Nancy Moore in 1814, Hanna owned a number of slaves, a "ropewalk," a stable and several pieces of business property and had just sold his interest in "Starling and Hanna—Merchants" to Anthony Hunn.

By February 1819, Hanna and William Fulkerson had bought Munday's one-half interest, and now Hanna, during the watering season of 1819, owned three-fourths of the valuable Greenville Springs property—more than any other one person had owned since its beginning as a spa. Hanna's grandiose ideas, uncertain statewide financial conditions and a rival spa in Harrodsburg all spelled trouble ahead. Even rising costs of foodstuffs were a factor: beef was five cents per pound, butter eight cents, corn meal forty-four cents per bushel and chickens a dollar a dozen. Hanna proved to be incompetent as "host to the public." After selling the ropewalk, several of the town lots, the stable, a few slaves and two business buildings to pay for the Greenville Springs, he and Fulkerson mortgaged this valuable property to Robert Boyce for $13,000. Boyce was eventually repaid all but $3,800.[28]

Certainly, the public was not aware of these business affairs, and for two seasons, Greenville Springs drew an overflow crowd. During this time, several new entertainment establishments opened in Harrodsburg. James Higgins opened the Harrodsburg Inn on Main Street, John Chiles ran his Tavern in Morgan Row behind the courthouse and there was also Robards Tavern, Eccles Tavern and Millers Tavern—each catered to visitors who came to Harrodsburg to "take the waters." An advertisement in the Danville newspaper, the *Olive Branch*, on May 19, 1820, confirms this:

> *Harrodsburg Inn—J. Higgins*
> *Takes this opportunity of informing the people of Kentucky, that he has opened a*
> *House of Entertainment*
>
> *At the stand formerly kept by Mr. Thomas Hooe, Main Street; where he has every arrangement for taking boarders, who may visit the Greenville Springs. The springs are situated about half a mile from his house, which is an agreeable walk at any time of the day. His prices of boarding, stabling, etc., are no higher than the usual prices thro' the state. He humbly solicits a share of the public patronage, under the consideration that he is enable to render satisfaction.*

Unfortunately, business affairs at Greenville Springs were going from bad to worse. Fulkerson gave Hanna his power of attorney to expedite matters, and Hanna in turn asked his friend Thomas P. Moore to act as his lawyer and to try to straighten out his business affairs. Hanna sold or mortgaged the rest of his property; he borrowed money from his friends and from the Bank of Kentucky with Silas Harlan, Samuel Taylor and Robert Mosley as surety; and he mortgaged his slaves to Daniel Brewer. He did everything he could to forestall financial failure.[29]

Greenville Springs.

FROM reports which have been put into circulation respecting the entertainment at the Greenville Springs representing the rates to be extravagant and unreasonable, great injustice has been done to the proprietor, who has been making every preperation to render the entertainment not only comfortable but elegant, and has made arrangements to accommodate a large number of visitants u on the most reasonable terms.

The following are the prices charged.

RATES OF BOARDING, &c.

	SPECIE.
Lady or Gentleman per month, - - -	$16 00
Do. Do. per week, - - -	4 50
Children and Servants, half price.	
Keeping Horse per month, - - - -	6 00
Do. Do per week, - - - -	1 75

Any current bank notes will be received at their value. AMOS EDWARDS

August 9, 1823.—33-3t.

A newspaper clipping of Greenville Springs from the *Kentucky Gazette*, September 14, 1823. *Author's collection.*

Montgomery Bell, who had not been paid in full by Hanna for the original purchase, and Robert Boyce, who held the first mortgage on Greenville Springs, both plagued Hanna and filed suits in the October term of the Mercer Circuit Court in 1822 threatening foreclose. They claimed, "Hanna is now no inhabitant of this Commonwealth, and possibly not of these United States." At his wits' end, Hanna wrote from Tennessee, where he was visiting family, and said flatly, "Go on and foreclose." The sale was advertised on the tavern doors in Harrodsburg and in two central Kentucky newspapers, *Argus of Western America* in Frankfort and *Olive Branch* in Danville. Bell "bought-in" the property and no actual sale took place that summer, but the property was leased to two out-of-town managers, who ran this advertisement in the *Frankfort Commentator* on April 24, 1824:

> *Greenville Springs—Hiram C. Bennett and John Trimble*
> *Have recently obtained this celebrated watering place and intend at an early Period to open them for the reception of company. Having put the houses in complete repair, and it being one of the most comfortable situations for the convenience of those who may think property to visit this place either for the purpose of pleasure or the restoration of health; they can with confidence recommend the accommodations. The celebrity of this place and the medicinal qualities of its waters are too well known to require comment, and the order and regularity with which the house will be conducted will insure to the invalid and convalescent, comfort, and repose. Every article furnished at the Springs will be of the first quality and every exertion will be made to produce a plentiful supply of every luxury in season.*
>
> *The House will be under the immediate direction of Mr. Bennet. The following will be the terms of the House:*
>
> | | |
> |---|---|
> | *Boarding per Week* | *$4.00 in Specie* |
> | *Boarding per Month* | *$16.00 in Specie* |

Children	*Half Price*
Horses, per Week	*$1.50 in Specie*
Horses, per Month	*$6.00 in Specie*

Hiram C. Bennett
John Trimble

A stagecoach system—set up with good carriages, horses and a careful driver—ran once a week during the season between Lexington and Greenville Springs. There was a regular theatrical company of respectable performers during the season, and the best music available was furnished for "balls and private parties."

By the next year, Hanna had found a purchaser, he thought, for Greenville Springs. Amos Edwards of Jefferson County offered $30,000 for the property, and the deed was made on October 22, 1825. Part of the payment was a mortgage that Edwards held on a large tract of land in Logan County. Hanna was overjoyed and moved with his family to Montgomery County, Tennessee, after Edwards and his "hydropathic physician" assistant, Dr. Daniel M. Heard, came to take over the Greenville Springs. "Nature's benign remedy prepared by his own hand," "renovate both body and mind" and "an exhilarating effect upon a feeble constitution when taken in any considerable quantity" were the claims made by these two in the press of central Kentucky.[30]

This did not prove to be a successful season. Samuel Davis and Joel P. Williams, acting as lawyers for Hanna, could not collect money on the Logan County mortgage. Edwards felt cheated

Top: The state historical marker for Greenville Springs. *Keith Rightmyer.*

Bottom: An old, dry spring from the original Greenville Springs, located on the Beaumont Inn compound. *Helen Dedman.*

at the price he paid, and he sued to rescind the contract. Bell and Boyce still wanted their money, and a completely disgusted Hanna empowered a group of his friends—William Harrison, John and George Briscoe, Abraham Fulkerson, Thomas P. Moore, Samuel Davis and Joel P. Williams—to collect what notes and mortgages were due him, to pay off what debts they could and to try to straighten up the entangled financial affairs of Greenville Springs.

Greenville Springs Auctioned Off to Highest Bidder

The group tried to straighten up the financial affairs, but too many creditors were involved and they could not forestall an execution of the Mercer Circuit Court, which empowered Samuel McCoun, sheriff of Mercer County, to "levy an execution upon the Greenville Springs tract of land and to duly advertise and expose to public sale on the premises on November 23, 1826, said property."

For $4,843, Dr. Christopher C. Graham, as highest bidder, acquired the entire 227 acres of the Greenville Springs property, the tavern, all other buildings, the use of the name and the mineral rights to the several spring outlets. Hanna's friends gave a deed to Graham on February 9, 1827, but it wasn't until 1832 that all arguments were settled so Hanna could give a final deed.

Pauline Goddard Dedman, Sam Cooke, Hugh Crozer, Anna Chinn and Mary Lafon, all of Harrodsburg, helped in placing the location of "several spring outlets" on the Greenville Springs property. The largest and most famous of the springs can still be found in the brush and undergrowth of the field beyond the back fence near Chestnut Street. The "Fairy Dell," which has been filled in and covered over, was south of the swimming pool for the present Beaumont Inn. A third area was covered over when the present road was built on Elizabeth Court, and a fourth can be found on the "spring lot" on McBrayer Drive. At the time these springs were used, they had stone-walled sides built around the spring itself, the water flowed into a stone trench or basin and each was covered with an octagonal roof and lattice sides.

Much had happened at Greenville Springs. Harrodsburg had acquired a national reputation as a health resort, its businessmen had profited from visitors to the springs and invalids had felt improved in health. Extravagant parties and balls were enjoyed by families of guests, and many young people meeting at the spa later married, so there were lasting ties with various parts of the United States. Politics and business have been discussed and important decisions resolved, so some sadness prevailed when Greenville Springs went out of business. This did not last long. The new purchaser was the well-liked and industrious young owner-manager of the rival Harrodsburg Springs. With the two properties adjoining, Graham had no intention of trying to maintain the rival to his Harrodsburg Springs, so Greenville was absorbed and both properties became known as Graham Springs.

In May 1830, Graham practically gave away the tavern and main building, together with twenty-four acres of land—twelve acres on the west side of the Harrodsburg-Danville road including the buildings and twelve acres across the road including the "ropewalk" established by Bell and Eastland—to Reverend William D. Jones. This Baptist minister of Danville assisted in establishing a "Female Seminary of Learning on land embracing the site and buildings of the late Greenville Springs."[31]

The Opening of Greenville Institute for Young Ladies

Even though "the young lady scholars" were able to enjoy the use of the mineral waters at both Greenville and Harrodsburg Springs, Reverend William D. Jones had to agree to "take in no boarders," establish no "House of Entertainment for public use of the mineral waters" and return to Graham "any title for mineral spring that might hereinafter be discovered on the property." According to Graham, this land was given to Jones, but the deed shows that Jones paid the price of $1,000. At most this "seminary" lasted three sessions because in May 1834, Jones was living in Washington County; he had sold the property to the prominent Harrodsburg lawyer, James Harlan, for $1,425.[32]

When the Harlan family moved to Frankfort in 1841, the property was leased to Professor Samuel G. Mullins, who chartered and established an excellent school for girls called Greenville Institute for Young Ladies. So successful was Mullins that by 1849, he had purchased the twenty-four-acre site of his school from Harlan and added twenty-three acres more of the original Greenville Springs property by purchasing from Graham.

The course of instructions at this school embraced the ordinary English courses, including the study of the Bible and natural science, "for such

GREENVILLE INSTITUTE
FOR YOUNG LADIES,
NEAR HARRODSBURG, KENTUCKY.

THE eighteenth annual session will commence on the 25th of August next.

FACULTY.

SAMUEL G MULLINS, A.M., Principal.
HENRY H. WHITE, A.M., Vice Principal.
CARL FRITZ, Professor of Music.

The Preparatory Department is under the charge of an accomplished and experienced Teacher.

TERMS, PER SESSION OF TWENTY WEEKS.

Tuition in all the branches of the regular course, including Vocal Music, with board, washing, fuel, light and stationery, $70 in advance, or $75 if payment be delayed till the middle or close of the session

Lessons on the Piano or Guitar, with use of instruments, $28 in advance, or $30 if not paid before the middle or close of the session.

French, German, Drawing and Painting, $10 each

No extra charge for instruction in the Ancient Languages.

Sunday Uniform for Winter—Scarlet Merino Dresses, long white Aprons, and white Sun-bonnets trimmed with scarlet lutestring ribbon.

Sunday Uniform for Summer—Pink Dresses, with Aprons and Bonnets like those used in winter.

For Ordinary Use—Clothing of any description to suit the taste of the pupil. jy24 d6&wtsep1

REFERENCES—A. L. Shotwell, William Terry, Samuel Deyes, W. L. Prather, Elder H. T. Anderson, and members of the Christian Church generally.

A newspaper clipping about the Greenville Institute for Young Ladies from the *Louisville Daily Courier*, July 24, 1851. *Author's collection.*

A group of students from the Greenville Institute for Young Ladies in 1886. *Harrodsburg Historical Society.*

GREENVILLE INSTITUTE,
HARRODSBURG, KY.

THE 24th Session will commence on the 1st Monday in September next, and continue forty weeks without intermission.

Terms—in advance:

Board and Tuition..$150 00
Music on Piano or Guitar..........................56 00
French..20 00

jy13 d2&w1 S. G. MULLINS, Principal.

A newspaper clipping for the Greenville Institute from the *Louisville Daily Courier*, July 13, 1854. *Author's collection.*

young ladies as may desire a more vigorous mental discipline." It also offered regular college courses, including Latin and Greek and the usual mathematics. It had departments for French, drawing and painting, as well as instrumental and vocal music.[33]

The following is an 1854 advertisement from the *Courier-Journal*:

> *The tenth session of the Greenville Institute for Young Ladies will commence on the 7th of July 1845 and continue twenty-one weeks. S.G. Mullins, Principal; H.H. White, Professor of Mathematics; Jno. C. Dr. Salomon, Professor of Music. Terms in advance:*
>
> *Tuition, with stationery $20*
> *Instruction in Music (instrumental and vocal) with use of pianos $30*
> *Board, washing, fuel, and lights $50*
> *French, Waxwork, and Painting $8 each*
>
> *Means for defraying incidental expenses must be deposited with the Principal. Uniform for the warm season: pink gingham or calico dresses, white aprons, and white cambric sun bonnets; for the cold season: dark green merino dresses, white aprons, and green gingham sun bonnets. To this all must conform. No fine clothing or jewelry will be tolerated. Those wishing either to obtain or retain situations for their daughters or wards should always make application before bringing or sending them to the Institute. Fully satisfied that it is impossible to manage a large school with advantage, the Principal will not again allow the number of pupils to exceed fifty.*[34]

Parallel with Bacon College, the first college in Harrodsburg that in the decade of the 1840s was offering first-class college advantages for young men, the Greenville Institute offered a correspondingly high-grade school for young women. Whether advanced thought concerning the benefits of higher education for women or merely the foresight of an opportunity for better financial returns, it is not known why Mullins, in 1841, decided to resign from the chair of ancient languages in Bacon College to organize Greenville Institute. It is probable that both motives influenced him, but be that as it may, he rendered an inestimable service to the womanhood of this generation and those following.

Unfortunately, on May 19, 1851, fire struck the old building, and all visible remains of Greenville Springs were destroyed. Most of the furniture at the institute was able to be saved, but the loss was estimated between $7,000 and $8,000. There was no insurance on the property, so while the fire was still raging, Graham and his friend James Taylor collected enough subscriptions from the townspeople, approximately $3,000, to replace the old frame buildings with substantial brick buildings.[35]

According to the *Courier-Journal*:

> *Beriah Magoffin, Esq.,* [the twenty-first governor of Kentucky], *subscribed $1,000 to aid in rebuilding Greenville Institute. This is truly encouraging; and with such friends as the Institute has in this and many other counties in the State, we have every reason to hope that a sum sufficient to complete the work will soon be contributed. Meanwhile, the school is being conducted with it usual regularity.*[36]

The Greenville Springs College and Daughters College

After Mullins established the Greenville Institute at a cost of about $20,000, the school for the education of females successfully operated for ten years under the name and style of "Greenville Institute for Young Ladies." According to the *Kentucky Law Review*:

> *Be it enacted be the General Assembly of the Commonwealth of Kentucky, That said institution of learning shall be and it is hereby established and incorporated, under the name and style of the "Greenville Institute," and that John B. Bowman, Thomas J. Moore, ad John G. Handy, of Mercer*

County; Samuel Syres, of Boyle County; John Duncan, of Madison county; Joseph Bryand, and George W. Eelly, of Fayette county; George W. Trabue of Glasgow; H.T. Anderson, of Louisville; Thomas Welch of Crab Orchard; and W. Templeton Withers, of Cynthiana, and their successors in office, are hereby constituted a body politic and corporate, by the name and style of the trustees of the "Greenville Institute," by which name they shall have perpetual succession, and a common seal, with power to change the same at pleasure.[37]

According to the *Louisville Daily Courier*, the eighteenth annual session of Greenville Institute for Young Ladies commenced on August 25, 1853:

Faculty: Samuel G. Mullins, A.M., Principal
Henry H. White, A.M., Vice Principal
Carl Fritz, Professor of Music

The Preparatory Department is under the charge of an accomplished and experienced Teacher. Terms, per session of twenty weeks: tuition in all the branches of the regular course, including Vocal Music, with board, washing, fuel, light, and stationery, $70 in advance, or $75 if payment be delayed till the middle or close of the session. Lessons on the piano or guitar, with use of instruments, $28 in advance, or $30 if not paid before the middle or close of the session. French, German, Drawing and Painting $10 each. No extra charge for instruction in the Ancient Languages. Sunday Uniform for Winter—scarlet Merino dresses, long white aprons, and white sun bonnets trimmed with scarlet lutestring ribbon. Sunday Uniform for Summer—pink dresses, with aprons and bonnets like those used in winter. For Ordinary Use—clothing of any description to suit the taste of the pupil.

In 1856, the forty-seven-acre Greenville campus, with the newly completed brick structure, was purchased by Professor John Augustus Williams and his father, Dr. Charles Edward Williams. They established and ran Daughters College for thirty-seven years, drawing students from many states until 1893.

A catalogue from July 1856, containing the "Educational Announcement of Daughters College—C.E. and Jno. Aug. Williams, Proprietors," gives the branches of learning for the four year's course of that early date:

Freshman Class: Algebra, Ancient History, Natural Philosophy, English Grammar, Anatomy and Physiology, and daily lectures of an hour on "The Pentateuch" [the first five books of Jewish and Christian scriptures].

Left: A portrait of John Augustus Williams, president and founder of Daughters College. *Harrodsburg Historical Society*.

Right: This is an early advertisement for Daughters College. *Beaumont Inn Collection*.

> *Sophomore Class: Geometry, Middle Ages, Composition, Rhetoric, Chemistry, Zoology, and lectures on Old Scriptures.*
> *Junior Class: Modern History, Trigonometry, Astronomy, Logic, Botany, Geology, and daily recitations on The Gospels.*
> *Senior Class: Ethics, English Classics, U. S. Constitution, Political Economy, Intellectual Philosophy, Book-keeping, and lectures on Acts of the Apostles. This was a full course, even measured by the curriculum of the present day.*

A later catalogue added to the curriculum "an optional course in Analytical Chemistry, Telegraphy, Taxidermy, Drawing, Music, Latin, French and Surveying." Other professional instructions stressed a course of reading for each course, declaring that "text-books alone, without much general reading, cannot educate properly. A taste for pure literature, the ability to read and the habit of research by means of the library are worth more to young women than the careless study of all textbooks in the world."

The Williamses emphasized that there must be "no extravagance in personal expenses, economy is a virtue, and extravagance worse than folly and neither wise nor genteel." They advocated neat, plain uniform of dress and to "dispense with every article of superfluous jewelry." Their uniform for the young ladies was as follows:

> *For summer, pink lawn or calico dresses are worn; white jaconet aprons, waist or long; white sun bonnets with splits trimmed in blue. For winter, green woolen dresses, dark aprons, and green hoods made for warmth and service. Further on this point will be cheerfully furnished by the matrons, if desired. To this regulation, all pupils, except those in black, will strictly conform. Young ladies who matriculate in September, and whose summer wardrobe has been already furnished, will not be required, at this time, to incur the additional expense by adopting the summer costume.*[38]

The same catalogue also stated:

> *The whole expense of a young lady, including charges for board, fuel, light, washing, medical attention, collegiate instruction, home instruction, use of library and apparatus and vocal music, will not exceed one hundred*

Alumnae of the Daughters College class of 1880 posing for a reunion photograph. Annie Bell Goddard, founder of Beaumont Inn, is standing on the left-hand side. *Beaumont Inn Collection.*

and sixty dollars per annum, or for one collegiate year. Drawing, Painting, Needlework, Piano, Guitar at an additional cost of fifty dollars per annum. At the same time, the student may receive further instruction, if she chooses, in the practical business of housekeeping. No charge will be made, except for the ordinary rates of board.

Daughters College acquired the reputation of graduating the best-educated women of any institution. President Williams's educational methods were ahead of his time. His curriculum was short compared to the curriculum of women's colleges of today, but he did more than make the minds of his pupils storehouses of knowledge. He taught them to think, and they entered the world with confidence and power. One of his teachers, a graduate of his college, declared that the secret of Mr. Williams's success was his extraordinary ability to impress on his pupils the ideals and aspirations for a fuller, rich life. This caused him to be remembered by his graduates through the years, and they sent their own daughters to the college.[39]

During the 1893–94 school session, Dr. James M. Dalton and Miss Ovie Smedley ran the school under the name Greenville Springs College. In the fall of 1894, Colonel Thomas Smith, veteran of the army of the Confederate States of America, bought the school and successfully ran it under the name of Beaumont College for twenty-three years.

A group of students from Beaumont College in 1915 or 1916. *Harrodsburg Historical Society.*

Beaumont College, Harrodsburg, Ky., (Successor to Daughters' College)
Pub. by Britton Music Co., Harrodsburg, Ky.

A historical postcard of Beaumont College, the successor to Daughters College. *Author's collection.*

When this Beaumont College closed in 1917, Glave and Annie Bell Goddard and May Pettibone Hardin purchased the property for $7,500, but soon after, the Goddards became the sole owners and opened Beaumont Inn to the public. Today, their descendants offer hospitality and fine accommodations to guests, without the use of the mineral springs, at the site of the once-famous Greenville Springs.[40]

Welcome to Historic Beaumont Inn

After Beaumont College was closed in 1917, the Goddards converted the property into the Beaumont Inn resort. More than a century later, descendants of the Goddards continue to refine the art of southern hospitality. The estate resembles a park with many old hardwood trees, peacefully secluded from the modern world. The fourth and fifth generations of the family now open the doors of Beaumont Inn to welcome guests to their heritage and hospitality.

In addition to the Main Inn Building, which also houses the Old Owl Tavern and Owl's Nest Lounge, the Beaumont Inn compound includes Greystone House, Bell Cottage Spa and Goddard Hall. There is also a swimming pool and numerous local activities in which to participate.

Each room in the Main Inn is individually decorated with antique furnishings and has a private bath, high ceilings, cable television, wireless Internet access and central air conditioning. Guestrooms are located on the second and third floors. The parlors, dining room and gift shop are on the first floor. Diamond Rooms are the most spacious rooms in the Main Inn and feature a king bed, a sitting area and an electric fireplace. Gold Rooms are large corner rooms with two double beds or a king bed. Silver Rooms are just a bit smaller and feature a king or queen bed.

The Greystone House features four large bedrooms and was originally built in 1931 as a private residence adjoining the inn property. This gracious home has become an integral part of the inn, and some of the guestrooms have been recently renovated to include deluxe king-size beds, two-person whirlpool baths and "new technology."

Goddard Hall, named after Annie Bell Goddard, was built in 1935 and features ten deluxe guest rooms with queen-size beds. Two of the rooms have Murphy beds to sleep an extra person. Several of these rooms contain framed memorabilia and articles of clothing belonging to Goddard. It is a perfect place for a family reunion or small groups since it has great porches for gathering.

In the Bell Cottage, a smaller freestanding building, patrons can pamper the body and spirit at Beaumont Inn's Kentucky Spa. This lovely little spa

A historical postcard of Beaumont Inn, the newest inn in the oldest town, circa 1920. *Author's collection.*

A historical postcard of Beaumont Inn, circa 1940s. *Author's collection.*

offers a variety of broad-based treatments designed to relax, renew and rejuvenate through a serene and sensuous therapy experience. It offers Serenity Massage, Couple's Massage, Hot Stone Massage, Facial Massage and Hand and Foot Treatments.

For business meetings, business conferences or private banquets, Beaumont Inn offers the unique experience of genuine Kentucky tradition. The historic atmosphere and acclaimed reputation of the Dining Room offers a complete, comfortable and productive experience for meetings and small conferences. Business travelers can enjoy unwinding at the two bars, one in the Old Owl Tavern and one in the Owl's Nest. The John Augustus Williams Meeting Room offers many modern amenities, and the James Harrod Room is perfect for small, casual meetings and breakout meetings of up to twenty people.

The Owl's Nest features a cozy pub atmosphere complete with a small, intimate paneled bar and additional designer seating allowing for a most relaxing atmosphere to conclude the activities of the day. You can get a drink before or after your dinner at the Tavern or Main Dining Room. The English-style pub is intimate and great for a romantic evening or a gathering of friends and family.

For fans of Kentucky bourbon, the bourbon distilleries near Harrodsburg are a must-see. If you want to develop a taste for fine Kentucky bourbon, a

A photograph of the Owl's Nest Pub at Beaumont Inn. *Keith Rightmyer.*

personalized private Bourbon Tasting with Dixon Dedman at Beaumont Inn is the only way to go. They offer more than seventy-five different bourbons, and Dedman will take you through the taste profiles, history and nuances of up to six Kentucky bourbon as you taste together in the comfy confines of the inn's Tasting Room.

Kentucky is fortunate to have many talented artisans in state, and many are featured in the Beaumont Inn gift shop. They feature "Kentucky Crafted" items created by craftsmen who have been juried, or judged, by the Kentucky Arts Council. Many local artists are also represented in the shop, in the form of jewelry, pottery, weaving, oil paintings, watercolors and photography prints. The gift shop will also ship to you anything in the shop, including cookbooks, corn meal batter, cake mix, brown sugar, syrup and souvenirs.

Chapter 2

SUTTON/HARRODSBURG/ GRAHAM SPRINGS

1806–1853

Dr. Graham, the proprietor, keeps the house himself and feels an interest in maintaining the character of the establishment; which is evinced not only in the large sums which he has expended in improving and beautifying the property, but in his personal courtesy and his indefatigable attention to his guest.
—Martha Stephenson, "Old Graham Springs," Register of Kentucky State Historical Society *12, no. 34 (January 1914)*

Sutton Springs Become Harrodsburg Springs

There were many mineral springs along the Kentucky River, and in the early to mid-1800s, many "high-living" southerners could bring their sons and daughters—or other family members suffering from malaria-ridden blood, cholera or other health disorders—to recuperate in pleasant surroundings. Among these were Drennon, Franklin, Crab Orchard, Estill and Greenville Springs. These were chalybeate (iron salts) watering places, not hot water springs, and they attracted crowds of visitors each year. Every summer, Kentucky River boats unloaded crowds of frail strangers who came to seek physical restoration and pleasure by the side of the sulfur-laden waters. The most famous of all, however, was Graham Springs, owned by Dr. Christopher Columbus Graham. This gracious Kentucky gentleman completely mastered the delicate Kentucky art of making people feel at home.

Ten Years Annual Instalments.

THE subscriber offers for sale the following property in the Town of Harrodsburg, on the above terms:

A HOUSE AND LOT, occupying one of the principal corners for business. The house is well adapted to a store or a mechanic's front shop, with extensive dwellings attached.

A LOT OF TWO ACRES, on which is a horse mill, a carding factory, an oil press and a hat factory.

Also, the HARRODSBURG SPRINGS. This tract contains about 70 acres, and is known as one of the principal watering places in the State. On this last piece of property there would be some little money required, and that might be arranged without cash in hand. Let not the long credits induce a belief that the prices will be in proportion.

DAVID SUTTON.

Harrodsburg, November 26, 1827. 41–3mo

A newspaper clipping about David Sutton's Harrodsburg Springs from the *Kentucky Gazette*, November 26, 1827. *Author's collection.*

Harrodsburg has long been a tourism destination, and it began in the early 1800s, due primarily to the discovery of several mineral springs. These springs gave rise to several grand hotels, and Harrodsburg rapidly gained a reputation as the "Saratoga of the South." From 1806 to 1853, Harrodsburg's famous spas—Greenville Springs, Harrodsburg Springs, and Graham Springs—offered mineral water, gambling, horse racing and gala entertainment to crowds of summer visitors. These medicinal springs, less than one mile apart, have slight differences in their mineral makeup.

These springs were considered good for the bowels, kidneys, liver, digestion, appetite and skin, as well as being a laxative and sedative. The waters were used to cure indigestion, urinary disorders, skin diseases, dropsy (edema), rheumatism and bone and joint inflammations, and supposedly they even improved the mood and strength of the sick. However, it was also believed that these springs could aggravate heart and lung conditions.

From all recorded historical accounts, it appears that Graham came to Harrodsburg in 1819. He was newly married to Theresa Sutton, daughter of David Sutton, a successful local businessman. Because of this marriage, Graham acquired a small tract of land near Sutton Springs containing a second medicinal spring. In 1820, Graham and Sutton combined these two springs, and Sutton Springs became known as Harrodsburg Springs. This was the beginning of the crowning achievement of Graham's life and in the history of Harrodsburg.

Although Graham assisted with the operation of Harrodsburg Springs from the beginning, he did not become immersed in the spa business officially until he bought Greenville Springs in 1827. At the time, Graham's father-in-

N. B. *Ladies and Gentlemen* wishing to visit Sutton's Harrodsburg Springs, can be accommodated with Boarding on moderate terms. A STAGE will also run three times a week from Lexington through Harrodsburg to Danville. J. G. C.

Harrodsburg, July 12, 1825—28-3m

A newspaper clipping for Sutton's Harrodsburg Springs from the *Kentucky Reporter*, July 18, 1825. *Author's collection.*

law was the majority owner of Harrodsburg Springs. According to Richard C. Brown's "Graham Expanded Springs' Resort," when Graham bought Greenville Springs, he combined the two resorts into Harrodsburg Springs and set about improving his property. Graham was more than a welcoming host—he was a man of means and foresight.

Dr. Christopher C. Graham, Harrodsburg Entrepreneur

Graham was born in 1784 at Worthington's Station, near Danville, Kentucky, and he grew up around the rich country along the Kentucky River. He was given the same Christian names as his uncle, Christopher Columbus Worthington, who had established the station. His father, James, was an early explorer with the "Long Hunters," a group of pioneers who organized extended expeditions into the wilderness from the Virginia frontier.

Graham's boyhood was spent climbing through the deep ravines and up the rugged cliff sides of the steep river palisades. He was truly a product of the Kentucky frontier. When he was a young adult, many people claimed that he was the best rifle shot in the West, and Graham indeed won many shooting competitions. Added to his superior accomplishments with the rifle, he was also an able flatboat man. He made numerous trips to New Orleans piloting a flatboat loaded with Kentucky products for sale to French and other foreign buyers. In 1812, like most young American boys, he volunteered for the militia and served in the Detroit campaign.

In 1872, William Belknap Allen, the author of a *History of Kentucky*, devoted thirty-five pages of his work to a biography of Graham. He called

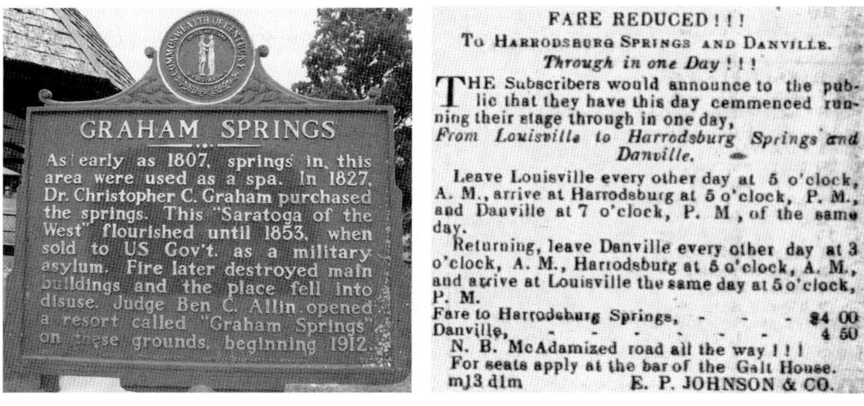

FARE REDUCED!!!
To HARRODSBURG SPRINGS AND DANVILLE.
Through in one Day!!!

THE Subscribers would announce to the public that they have this day cemmenced running their stage through in one day,
From Louisville to Harrodsburg Springs and Danville.

Leave Louisville every other day at 5 o'clock, A. M., arrive at Harrodsburg at 5 o'clock, P. M., and Danville at 7 o'clock, P. M, of the same day.

Returning, leave Danville every other day at 3 o'clock, A. M., Harrodsburg at 5 o'clock, A. M., and arrive at Louisville the same day at 5 o'clock, P. M.

Fare to Harrodsburg Springs, - - - $4 00
Danville, - - - - - - - 4 50

N. B. McAdamized road all the way!!!
For seats apply at the bar of the Galt House.
mj3 d1m E. P. JOHNSON & CO.

Left: The state historical marker for Graham Springs. *Keith Rightmyer.*

Right: A newspaper clipping for the Harrodsburg Springs stagecoach routes from the *Louisville Daily Journal*, May 18, 1844. *Author's collection.*

Graham a "living encyclopedia" of Kentucky history. According to friends who knew Graham, "He hunted with Daniel Boone, was an intimate friend of William Whitley, knew the family of Abraham Lincoln very well, and at the age of one hundred, could kill a turkey with a shot to the head without the aid of glasses."

When Graham was a child, afflictions such as indigestion, heartburn, gout, hypochondria, mania or rheumatism, as well as suicide, were unheard of. He learned early that "manly entertainments, simple food, and fresh air cured more aliments than all modern medicines." As a young adult, Graham did not use tobacco or stimulants, but later in life he did imbibe occasionally. With all his life experiences, Graham became a nineteenth-century expert of health.

Graham had many careers in his lifetime, but he remained dedicated to being a master marksman with his favorite gun, "Old Blucher." He formed the Boone Club and operated a rifle range at Graham Springs. At one time, the Boone Club, a local shooting club, offered a purse of $10,000 to anyone who could outshoot Graham. The challenge was published throughout the nation, as well as in Canada and a number of European nations. Because of Graham's reputation, no one accepted the challenge, and the club members declared him "the undisputed champion off-hand rifle shot."[41]

Graham owned a silversmith business in Springfield, Kentucky, before the War of 1812. When the military conflict intensified, he sold his shop and, with the profits from the sale, equipped a local group of volunteers into a militia. He served three years in the War of 1812 as a captain, suffered a wound during the Battle of Mackinaw and was captured twice, once by Canadians and once by Native Americans. He continued his military career during the Mexican War of Independence.

Graham graduated from Transylvania University Medical School with a degree in medicine and became its first graduate. He was an apprentice to pioneer surgeon Ben Dudley, an intense doctor who proved to be an excellent mentor for Graham. In 1819, after serving as a surgeon on Colonel Robert Gray's expedition to survey land for the Southern, Atlantic and Pacific Railroad, he arrived in Harrodsburg with twenty dollars and a medical education as his only way to make a living.

With a profitable marriage to the daughter of David Sutton and a shrewd business foresight, Graham made a national reputation for himself and his community—not in medicine, but in entertainment. He realized that the springs of Harrodsburg could be made "into an attractive resort to draw the attention of the people of the rapidly expanding West, and from those islands of cotton planting along the Mississippi River in the lower South."

After purchasing the land and mineral springs of Greenville Springs, Graham took several slaves with him to the Three Forks country up the Kentucky River, and they dug fine mountain shrubbery and trees for reforestation. In order to bring the plants back to Harrodsburg, they were drifted down the river on a flatboat to the Shaker ferry landing and then hauled in wagons to Harrodsburg. Graham was an excellent horticulturist, and he diligently searched the countryside around Harrodsburg, hunting for beautiful plants to bring to his grounds. He stated many times that he wished "to create the most beautiful park in America."[42]

Dr. Graham's role as a physician often put him at odds with the current fashions of the day. He often complained about the custom of women wearing restrictive corsets. "How can a fashionable lady with ribs crushed together and respiration thus obstructed, expect to enjoy health, or give constitution to her offspring?" Another feminine fashion he objected to was "not so injurious, but equally ludicrous…sticking of a peck of hair on the back of their heads (sweaty and ponderous to be borne), and all this to be crowned only with a droll, buffoonish looking thing [hat], giving to the face a most unnatural and farcical appearance."[43]

In Reuben T. Durrett's Christopher Columbus Graham Papers, 1860–1878, he stated that during Dr. Graham's life "he was devoted to the collection of items to preserve the natural history of Kentucky" and spent

Left: A photograph of Dr. Christopher Columbus Graham, owner of the Graham Springs Hotel. *Kentucky Historical Society.*

Below: This family gunpowder horn was passed down to Dr. Christopher C. Graham. *Mel Stewart Hankla.*

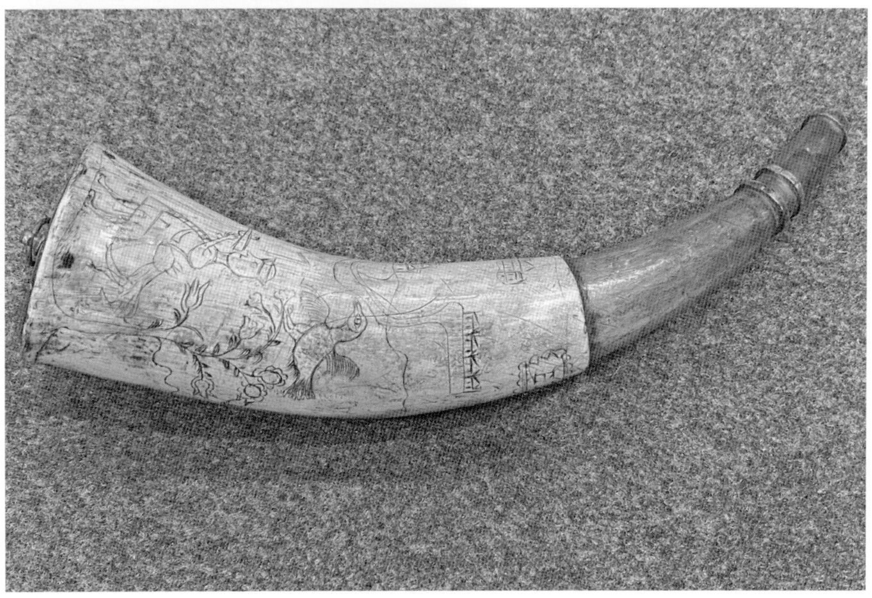

the latter years of his life "gathering specimens for the Louisville Museum." Graham is widely known to historians as "a physician, hunter explorer, surveyor, and author." He lived to be one hundred, and his centennial birthday was celebrated with a grand banquet at the Louisville Hotel. He died on February 3, 1885.

Dr. Graham Purchases Greenville Springs

Graham acquired the entire 227-acre tract of Greenville Springs at absolute auction when Mercer County foreclosed on the property in 1826. Not wanting to have two competing resorts in the same small town, Graham decided to combine the springs and the land and incorporate them into the newly named Graham Springs. In May 1830, Graham deeded all the Greenville Springs' buildings and 24 acres of land to Reverend William James for the establishment of a female seminary.

Graham's genius, personal charm and intelligent energy made this the most popular and famous resort of the South and Middle West, a mecca for invalids from many parts of the United States. His knowledge of industry led him to convert a ragged, treeless property into a landscaped garden of exquisite beauty adorned with native trees, shrubs and plants obtained from the Kentucky landscape.

According to Van Arsdall's "The Springs at Harrodsburg," the first things Graham built were substantial two-story frame houses and long rows of one-story cottages. Once this was completed, he erected an "extensive hotel and a magnificent ballroom of corresponding size, which could be seen miles away looming up in a beautiful setting of green." The hotel was a "full four stories high" with "a massy colonnade, rich capitals, and lofty entablature" and was said to be "the finest edifice in the West." The resort also included a fifty-by-one-hundred-foot ballroom, several bowling alleys, many nature walks, an artificial lake and "an elegant saloon for the accommodation of patients who may wish for other kinds of physical exercise," complete with all the embellishments. Graham announced that the springs were "now capable of accommodating one thousand persons, at the rate of Wealthy southerners came in splendid equipages with many servants as attendants." At the height of its popularity, Graham Springs would see from 4,000 to 6,000 visitors each season, sometimes 1,200 at a time.

Dr. Graham successfully operated his "Saratoga of the South," whose peak of success was in the late 1840s, as the most fashionable spa in Kentucky. Most of the early pioneers thought that the mineral springs were beneficial for all types of ailments. Wealthy families from the Deep South made the long trip by stagecoach and steamboat to "take the waters" to ward off disease. Women especially looked forward to the fancy dresses and masquerade balls that were popular during the social season.

Graham Springs encompassed approximately 280 acres, and with the new improvements, it became "an establishment so extensive that when

The only known lithograph of the historic Graham Springs Hotel, built by Dr. Christopher Columbus Graham. *Kentucky Historical Society.*

illuminated at night it might be seen for miles," according to Nathaniel Parker Willis. Describing his reaction to Graham Springs the evening of his arrival, Nathaniel Nathan Willis concluded that "I had stumbled upon a most unexpected mixture of paradise and public-house." Lewis Collins's *Historical Sketches of Kentucky* adds more to the description of Graham Springs:

> *The grounds are elevated and extensive; adorned with every variety of shrubbery grown in America, interspersed with some of the most beautiful and rare exotics from Europe and Asia, and traversed by wide gravel walks, intersecting, and crossing each other in every direction. A small and beautiful lake, three hundred yards long, one hundred yards in width, and fifteen feet deep, lately excavated, is well stored with fish of the finest flavor, and its glassy surface enlivened by the presence of many wild and tame waterfowls.*

The Success of Graham Springs Resort

On June 16, 1841, more than ten thousand people met at Graham Springs to celebrate the sixty-seventh anniversary of the founding of Harrodsburg. Tourists and military companies "flocked in from all the neighboring towns and paraded up and down the famous tanbark [oak tree] walk." The majority of overnight participants stayed at the Graham Springs Hotel.[44]

Dashing militia captains strutted their companies back and forth on the parade ground near Graham Springs. Among the units present were Lexington Rifle Infantry, Versailles Artillery, Frankfort Light Infantry, Georgetown Artillery, Danville Artillery, Harrodsburg Central Guards, Cloverbottom Rifleman, Athens Greys and Jessamine Cavalry. Former attorney general of Kentucky (1832–38) and future governor Charles Morehead (1855–59) was there to inspect the troops and shake hands with the citizens of the state.

Hundreds of southerners were on hand to intermingle with the cheerful Kentuckians in their proud moment of celebrating the foundation of the first settlement of the state. "Kitchen Knife Ben" Hardin delivered the keynote address. Hardin was a leading Kentucky lecturer and humorist. In a vein of true Kentucky philosophy, he observed that "three things are mighty uncertain, who a woman will marry, what horse will win the race, and which way a jury will decide."[45]

In 1845, the editor of the *Frankfort Commonwealth* visited Graham Springs and came home to write about it:

> *To those who have never been there a single word would be superfluous, but to those who have not, we are justified in saying they will find mineral water whose medical properties are highly beneficial; trees, and shades and lawns and shrubberies, and walks, that Shenstone might have envied; architecture of the English rural cottage order and noble Grecian; music as sweet as the voice of birds, or the laugh of fresh-lipped girls; society, men and women, the elite of this great and intelligent continental accommodations, the most agreeable and sumptuous that skill, taste, and liberality can provide, enjoyment to the highest bent, whether you prefer fashionable bustle or rural seclusion; host highbred, attentive amicable and liberal; in short everything that the heart may wish at such a place. Such is a just tribute as we know by experience.*

When the Graham Springs property had expanded to 280 acres by 1850, it included an artificial lake, a grotto, an icehouse, an aqueduct and reservoir, walking and riding paths, three additional bowling alleys, bathhouses, warm showers and steam rooms, whole avenues of private cottages for wealthy guests and a boardwalk through a grove of locust trees leading from the hotel to the springs. Octagonal gazebos stood atop the springhouses at the

A historical postcard of the artificial lake located at Graham Springs. *Author's collection.*

Saloon Spring and Graham Springs. Water was carried by employees from the springs to "treatment rooms" at the hotel, equipped with showers and tub baths.

A "professor of dancing" was hired to conduct cotillion parties with fancy dress and masquerade balls. These were held in the two ballrooms, and Graham owned a band of slave musicians who provided entertainment at the springs during the summer months and were hired out to perform in Louisville during the winter months.

Graham Springs Hotel entertained many important and famous people before the Civil War. It is said that the guest register books held the names of everyone who ever visited. One of these guest books was used in a murder trial in the 1850s to locate the whereabouts of certain witnesses at the time of the murder.

Graham Spring was an ideal place to fall in love, and one of Judge John Rowan's daughters did in 1829. She left her famous home in Bardstown to enjoy the pleasures of Harrodsburg. In a surge of wild, romantic passion, she wrote to a girlfriend in Frankfort, "I should have written you sooner, but I have not had a moment, and it is now 1 o'clock and I have just left the ballroom. If I could only describe to you this lovely place, the many comforts, and luxuries we have, together with the interesting gentlemen."

Miss Rowan soon learned that "there were two gentlemen worth more than a million apiece." She continued in her letter about other exciting news: "The table is the best I ever sat down to at any place: Ice Cream in profusion. The cottages are furnished beautifully. All of them with large closets."[46]

Nathaniel Parker Willis in his famous *Health Trip to the Tropics* went by Harrodsburg "to take the waters." He was fascinated by the continuous procession of expensive medical equipment, the property of wealthy southern families and the regal bronze lions guarding the entrance to the hotel. To Willis, as he observed this exciting resort crowd moving about him, Dr. Graham appeared an extremely hospitable host.

As an added note about the aforementioned regal bronze lions, when Graham Springs was dismantled by the U.S. government in the 1860s, these bronze lions were thrown into the man-made lake. The lake was eventually filled in, and during the mid-1900s, the Chestnut Street Apartments were built.

Sometimes humorous activities at the resort would backfire, leaving Graham in a precarious position. One warm summer evening before the supper meal, a group of visitors began playing with Graham's trained hunting dog. The men sat in a circle, and each took a turn giving the animal a glove so he would return it to the appropriate spouse. One confirmed bachelor gave a glove to the enthusiastic dog and asked him to deliver it to his wife, thinking the dog would be confused. The dog, however, ran out of the room and found one of the African American maids and handed her the glove. That evening at dinner, the bachelor was not invited to Dr. Graham's table.

In the evenings, when there were no grand balls, parties gathered in clusters under the sheltering oaks and thrilling stories were pasted around. The lemonade, "a delicious concoction of citrus fruit juice and a dash of rare old bourbon, kept tongues wagging, and happy laughter ringing throughout the grove."[47]

One evening, during a party under the trees, Noah Miller Ludlow, an actor who had been on the American stage for several years, and his companions enjoyed the heavily spiked beverages and matched stories with their host until late at night. They drank frequently from "the silver pitchers of Dr. Graham, and between puffs on long cigars they were led gaily along in their merrymaking." The lemonade, cigars, stories, "sweet young girls in crinoline, a seductive south wind, and gentle moonlight falling in big splotches through the sheltering oak branches," infected a romantic German visitor named Mr. Koumar.[48]

A historical postcard of Dr. Graham's Old Saloon Spring, located at Graham Springs. *Author's collection.*

The ladies in attendance at Graham Springs were excited with their "elaborately dressed hair" styles of "the New Orleans fashion," as the *Courier-Journal* noted on November 17, 1929, and the organdy and muslins of their ball gowns. In the mornings, ladies walked to the springs under the shade of the arching locust trees branches. The ballroom at night was a scene of charm, and it was obvious that Graham was the master of ceremonies and life of the party.

It was always exciting in Harrodsburg with the arrivals and departures of the stagecoaches. Visitors already at the springs would rush out to see what famous people were arriving or leaving. Young girls hurried down "to see if a prospective, handsome, and wealthy beau had arrived, and the young men to see if a new fair-haired charmer was on hand." Some of the many prominent "belles" who came to the springs were "Sally Ward and Fanny Smith of Louisville, Alice Corneal of Cincinnati, the Widow Shelby of Danville, the Preston girls of Lexington, and the Poignard daughters from St. Louis." Judge Rowan's and Judge Bibb's daughters were also on hand to stroll up and down the long promenade with interesting companions. Many of the beautiful women who came to Graham Springs with their families were also looking for romance. "Creole beauties from New Orleans added

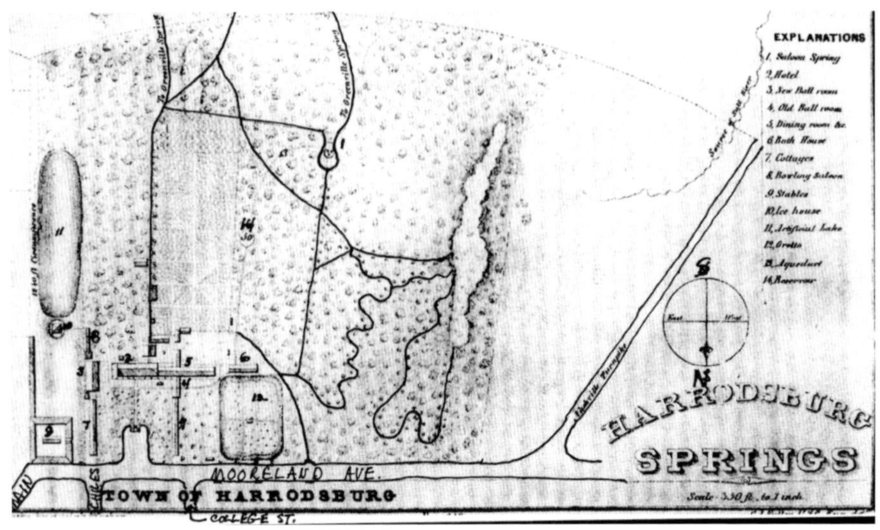

A map of the historic Graham Springs property. *Author's collection.*

charm and love interest to the great patches of moonlight which sifted down onto the spacious grounds." These exotic and dark-eyed beauties made the "moonlight and roses" of the South a happy reality.[49]

Among the male delegations visiting Harrodsburg were Kentucky political celebrities—Henry Clay, Robert Letcher, Colonel John Rown, Governor John Jordan Crittenden, George D. Prentice, William Graves, Robert J. Breckinridge, John S. Williams, William Preston and John Hunt Morgan. Numerous notable visitors came from outside Kentucky. One of these was the "flashy merchant prince, Glendy Burke, who followed sweet Alice Carneal there." Glendy was quite a handsome man in his day. Stephen Collins Foster wrote "a famous, black-faced minstrel" song entitled "Glendy Burke" in honor of the steamboat that bore the rich merchant's name. Frederick Peel, son of Sir Robert Peel, was also a frequent visitor, and he "caused considerable twittering among the ambitious mammas and their flirtatious daughters."[50]

After the death of his fourth wife, a grief-stricken colonel from Vicksburg arrived at Grahams Springs to recuperate and to forget about death and loss. The colonel's personal history, doubled with his grief, was noticeable to everyone around him. Only four beautiful girls, crowded into his "splendid coach," allowed him to make the journey and to ease his mourning. One lady wrote to her family about "the poor man who had four wives….[H]e is such a good man, a devout Methodist, he surely deserves a fifth." She also added that "he is so very rich."[51]

The cooling shade from the tree canopies allowed men to turn their conversations to subjects they thought important—horses, races and cards. Harrodsburg had a racetrack, Haggin Raceway, and during the height of the season, many race meets were held here. Kentuckians put their prize-winning horses against anyone from the rest of the South. When they got tired of horses and races, cards provided an adequate distraction. Among the many master card players to visit Graham Springs was the famous statesman Henry Clay.

Unfortunately, cockfighting was also a lively pastime at the resort, not only for honored veterans but also for brilliantly dressed southern belles and entourages of sons and daughters. Nathaniel Parker Willis recounts being

> *jostled along the road from Lexington to Harrodsburg with four companions who had a fine game fighter. The scarred warrior lay hobbled and panting on the floor of the stagecoach. He had just killed three bold antagonists in the nightstands at the Lexington track and was on his way to Harrodsburg to claim more victories. As they bobbed along, one of the sportsmen gave the garrulous Easterner a lesson in training a champion gamecock. "For three weeks afore the fight," said the cocksman, "feed the feller on egg, corn meal, rock candy and barley water." This, of course, was invaluable information to the effete New England man of letters.*

Many Kentuckians took advantage of the social season at Grahams Springs to foster trade between the regions. Many plantation owners fled the hot weather of the lower South to enjoy the social life of "likeminded" individuals. They also gathered under the shade of the giant oaks to make agricultural deals. They bought livestock from famous Kentucky cattle and horse breeders and hemp bagging to wrap their cotton bales. Cotton was very much on many Kentuckians' minds, and while Delta cotton plantation owners were visiting Graham Springs, they talked about land prices and the uncertain business of cotton planting.

Dr. Graham's Hunt for Three Runaway Slaves

The Nathan M. Ludlow Company played to large audiences in the grand ballroom. This company included Samuel, Douglas, James, Martha, Julia and Alexander Drake; John and Harry Vaught; Mr. Blisset; Mrs. Lewis; Miss Denny; and Ludlow. They remained at the springs for a month, and during this time they performed *A Dissertation on Faults*, *Alexander's Feasts*, *The Hunters of Kentucky*, *Alonzo and Imogene* and *The Day After the Fair*.

The professional actors also shared the entertainment spotlight with Dr. Graham's three musical slaves, who composed the Graham Orchestra. Reuben, Henry and George (no last names have ever been mentioned) had musical abilities that were well known throughout the South. For years, this orchestra played for the enchanting dances in the large ballroom at Graham Springs. When the resort season ended, Graham allowed the orchestra to go to Lexington and Louisville to play at other fashionable balls. Their services were in demand in the wealthy homes and on the Kentucky and Ohio steamboats. They played musical instruments with real talent, but they were also excellent waiters.

In 1841, "Old Tippecanoe" William Henry Harrison visited Lexington to confer with one of his Whig political advisers, Henry Clay. His "Log Cabin and Hard Cider Campaign" excited Kentuckians, and the citizens of Lexington wanted to give him a grand welcoming. Graham sent his musical waiters to assist in receiving the aged Whig warrior. The orchestra was placed under the supervision of a free man of color named Williams. After the reception in Lexington, the Graham Orchestra packed up their waiter's coats, music and instruments and went to Louisville, where they boarded the steamboat *Zebulon M. Pike* and headed for Canada.

At one time the Kentucky-Ohio border, like the one between Maryland and Pennsylvania, was one of the spawning grounds of fugitive slave cases "as enterprising slaves sought to escape across the Ohio River from Kentucky to Cincinnati and other southern Ohio towns. Once in Ohio, the slaves attempted to find their way north into Canada."[52]

In a doctrinal predecessor to the *Dred Scott* decision, *Strader v. Graham* would come to the Taney Court in 1850 (the Supreme Court of the United States from 1836 to 1864, when Roger Taney served as the fifth chief justice). The court's antebellum fugitive slave resolution of *Strader v. Graham* is seen as an effort to avoid the earthshaking constitutional issues affecting slavery and regional conflict. A closer look at *Strader v. Graham* reveals that many of the *Dred Scott* issues were not only raised but also addressed by the Taney Court justices.[53]

Sometime in January or February 1841, George, Reuben and Henry, together with another slave, boarded the steamboat *Pike* in Louisville for a trip up the Ohio River. At this time, the Ohio River was an established line between free and slave territories in the trans-Appalachian west. The Northwest Ordinance had "also provided that fugitive slaves who entered the Northwest Territory could be reclaimed and returned to their owners."[54] When Ohio and Indiana entered the Union in 1803 and 1816, respectively, their constitutions contained provisions banning slavery, identical in wording to the provision in the Northwest Ordinance.

Although steamboat owner Jacob Strader and his partner, James Gorman, were not able to establish that George had ever been taken into Ohio or Indiana, Graham's letter to Williams "demonstrated that both Reuben and Henry had entered formerly free territory that had become free states."[55] Both men returned to Kentucky after their brief visits and continued in Graham's employment. This distinction was crucial to the case, because if they had become free once they touched Ohio or Indiana soil, they were not "persons of color" within the meaning of the 1824 and 1827 Kentucky statutes.

Additionally, according to the laws of Ohio or Indiana, if the highest court of Kentucky eventually found that Reuben and Henry were not free when they returned to Kentucky, these findings would have serious consequences. This kind of final judgment by the state's highest court would invalidate a federal statute and would trigger review by the Supreme Court under Section 25 of the Judiciary Act of 1789.

From the moment Graham brought his bill of equity to Louisville chancery court, it was apparent that both sides were prepared to take *Strader v. Graham* as far as it could go in the courts. In a chancery court, a judge can order acts performed, such as modifying a contract or stopping an activity. The chancery court's functions are distinct from those of common law courts, which can order money damages to be paid and where jury trials are available.

After hearing evidence, Chancellor George Bibb dismissed the claims related to Reuben and Henry on the grounds that Graham's 1837 letter to Williams was the equivalent of "permission" to the owners of the *Pike* to transport them out of Kentucky. There was no mention of George in the letter, so Bibb allowed that claim go to a jury, which returned a verdict for Graham and fixed the damages at $1,000. Both sides appealed to the Kentucky Court of Appeals, seeking new trials. Graham argued that the damages awarded in Bibb's court were inadequate, and Strader argued that several damaging errors had been committed.[56]

In March 1844, Bibb's decision and the jury verdict were rendered, and for the next three and a half years, the litigation involving Graham and Strader moved from one Kentucky court to another, with both parties seeking every appeal available. In an opinion written by Chief Judge Thomas Marshall, the Kentucky Court of Appeals favored Graham on all points. By the time this case bounced from Bibb's court to the court of appeals and back again, the new court judge was Samuel Nicholas. The case was sent to a second jury, which again found for Graham, this time awarding him $3,000 in damages. It was appealed a second time to the court of appeals. After hearing two sets of oral argument over a period of nearly two years, "the court of appeals upheld Nicholas's decree ratifying the second jury's award."[57]

Two related concerns involving slavery and federalism were raised by the lawyers representing Graham and Strader in their successive appeals. Did a person holding the legal status of slave in Kentucky became free if he or she were transported to any free state and then returned to Kentucky? Did a slave become free if transported to a state whose territory was formerly part of the federal Northwest Territory, which was still present in the 1840s?

The difference between those two issues was vital for both sides in *Strader v. Graham*. As part of the federal policy on slavery in place in the 1840s, both slave and free states would afford "comity to the other laws on slavery, including the decisions of courts." This meant that if the Kentucky courts had "a rule that when the slave of a Kentucky resident traveled to a free state and returned to Kentucky, slave status 're-attached' on the return, the free state the slave had entered would acknowledge the legitimacy of that rule."[58]

Graham Springs Editorial Opinion from the *Courier-Journal*

During the mid- to late nineteenth century, many newspapers ran stories and editorials about Graham Springs. A few will be highlighted in this section. The following is an editorial opinion that was printed in the *Courier-Journal* on July 19, 1851:

> *Graham Springs Hotel stands upon a beautiful, wooded hilltop overlooking the historic town of Harrodsburg, itself one of the oldest and most famous resort hotels in the South.*
>
> *Twenty-five acres of almost virgin forestry surround it, in unusual beauty of location, its site superb, and its outlook majestic. As the changing seasons come and go in Kentucky, they write a progressive record of the sylvan beauty upon these woods that thrill an observer with the sheer loveliness of it. The bluegrass has a marvelous power of resurrection which no amount of scorching in summer drouths* [sic] *can destroy, and late rains of the fall*

season have laid an aftermath of tender green upon the sunlit slopes of Graham Springs woods Upon walnut trees of unusual size and symmetry dark clumps of mistletoe hang in profusion, their waxen berries turning to pearl in a setting of shimmering dark green leaves. It is no wonder that the Druids worshipped the mistletoe, with its suggestion of everlasting life! From oak and elm and walnut trees, brilliant autumn colors are flaunted in the face of on-coming winter, with a brave abandon. As one by one, scarlet, gold and russet-brown leaves float softly to earth, in the sill sunlight, sense of peace and restfulness falls like soothing balm upon the spirit of anyone who may walk there.

In 1820, Dr. C.C. Graham erected a classic building resembling an old-world castle upon these grounds, close to the famous Graham Springs, whose marvelous curative waters still attract people in search of health and pleasure. It does not need a page from the United States Dispensary, which states that, "Graham Springs and Saratoga are the only saline waters of true worth to be found in America," to convince one who has tasted it. May have declared it equal to the waters at Baden-Baden. Kentucky has an asset in this mineral water which she cannot afford to overlook, and progress will surely present it to the world in the fullest measure. In 1865, that year of the War Between the States anguish, the old hotel was burned. Its romantic memories, its charm and prestige, however, which are things of spiritual permanence, still cling about the place.

It was in Harrodsburg that George Rogers Clark planned his famous army for the conquest of the Northwest, in commemoration of which event. Old Fort Harrod has been made a State park. It was within the hotel grounds that a beautiful pageant, representing the early history of Kentucky, was given in celebration of the centennial anniversary of the founding of Harrodsburg, several years ago. A priceless old record book of Graham Springs Hotel shows names of men famous in the making of America. Henry Clay was a frequent guest and left his name upon its register. Pages might be printed of other famous signatures found there.

Old Dr. Graham himself, with his snow-white beard and princely bearing, was a conspicuous figure in the annals of Kentucky, not only leaving a record of his fame at Graham Springs, but at old Transylvania University at Lexington, where he received his education. Dr. Ephraim McDowell at Danville, and Dr. C.C. Graham at Harrodsburg were men who measured up to the highest standards in the world's medical records. The wise old doctor saw to it that his guest had a full measure of exercise and pleasure as well as curative waters to tone up the human system. A series of dances were inaugurated at Graham Springs before the War Between the States, which became famous for their brilliancy and aristocratic patronage. The musicians were colored slaves of Dr. Graham, highly trained and gaily liveried. The singing of "spirituals" before an audience began, in the old South, upon these occasions.

To this day the weekly dances at Graham Springs are social events of importance in Kentucky, during the season. Perhaps a mention of the antebellum balls may not be complete without reference to the beautiful "Unknown" who danced so gaily and so long at one of them, that she died of a heart attack on the same summer night. Her grave marked first by Dr. Graham, and afterward by the City of Harrodsburg, is shown to tourists who never fail to respond to the pathetic appeal of her story.

Mrs. James Harrod, widow of the hardy old pioneer who founded Harrodsburg, lived to an incredibly old age, and was an honored guest at Graham Springs on the first anniversary celebration held there.

On July 19, 1851, the *Courier-Journal* gave a rousing description of the ballroom dancing at the Graham Springs Hotel ballroom:

Returning from the ballroom, brilliantly illuminated by the sparkling eyes, rivaling the stars in their dazzling brilliancy, methought, if in the cool evening zephyrs that continually fanned my brown, (such were a possibility) to collect, my thoughts scattered in the whirring waltz, to the northern extremity of my brain. Truly the poet says there's a "magical influence in the wafted breeze"; but I am afraid (like the charming coquette) she has her favorites, for in spite of all my efforts, my thoughts continue to revert to the ball room! What a potent charm there is in the dance, and how delightfully sounds the music.

Graham Springs Sold to U.S. Government for Military Asylum

The reason Graham sold the Graham Springs property to the U.S. government in May 1853 is not clear in the historic literature. The government purchased the compound consisting of all the buildings for $100,000 to use as the Western Military Asylum, a military asylum used for "aged and invalid soldiers." Graham only sold 203 acres, keeping 25 acres for himself. It is unclear what happened to the remaining 50 acres.

THE WESTERN MILITARY ASYLUM.—The selection of the Harrodsburg Springs, with two hundred acres attached, for the site of the proposed western military asylum, in preference to the Blue Licks, gives eminent dissatisfaction to the friends of the latter locality now in Washington The wags are insisting, in fact, that the General's mortal aversion to these same Blue Licks settled the question in favor of Harrodsburg at $100,000; though the Licks aforesaid, with four hundred acres attached, were offered for $80,000 It seems to be estimated that the Harrodsburg site is worth in open market some $50,000. If so, Uncle Sam has come off better in this trade than in the purchase of a site for the Memphis Navy Yard, having to pay only twice as much as the property is really worth. However, fifty thousand here or there, is a mere circumstance to the Government in the matter of getting the very best possible location for such an establishment.

A newspaper clipping for the Western Military Asylum from the *Louisville Daily Courier*, May 14, 1953. *Author's collection.*

Fire destroyed the main buildings in 1859, and the patients were moved to a Washington, D.C., asylum. Two years later, it was sold for $120,000 to Captain Philip Thompson, who intended to turn the property back into a health resort. This dream was spoiled by the outbreak of the Civil War.

In 1862, the ballroom of the old Graham Springs was used as an operating room, and cottages were used as a hospital for wounded soldiers coming from the Battle of Perryville. Many of the buildings burned during the war, after which the grounds were converted to pastures and rented out by the federal government. When the beautiful hotel burned on May 30, 1856, and after the Battle of Perryville on October 8, 1862, the last vestige of the original Graham Springs disappeared.

In 1887, the property was auctioned for $19,001 to Edgar H. Gaither who, in turn, sold it to the Kentucky Real Estate and Improvement Association the following year.

THE LONE GRAVE MARKER

A lone, battered grave marker on the grounds of the former Graham Springs Hotel, now Youngs Park, is associated with Dr. Graham's era. A young woman died at Graham Springs and was buried under an unmarked stone in the trees near the Saloon Spring, within sight of the hotel. The grave has long been a source of local ghost stories.

For more than 150 years, this grave has been an object of the most imaginative speculation. It is more of a marker for the "good old days" of

"The Lone Grove'' by the Graham Springs. Its Occupant, a Beautiful Stranger, Dropped Dead in the Ball-room of the Springs Hotel, Back in the Forties. During the Excitement Her Handsome Partner, with Whom She Danced Each Set, Disappeared, Along with the Carriage in Which They Had Come.

A lone grave marking a mysterious death at Graham Springs Hotel. Local legend says that an unknown lady arrived at the hotel and then danced herself to death in the grand ballroom. *Author's collection.*

Graham Springs than for the human bones beneath it. The story behind this mysterious stone concerns a headstrong southern belle who came to Graham Springs to "take the waters" and died on Dr. Graham's dance floor during a lavish ball.

Historians recall that an unknown young girl arrived and signed the register as Miss Virginia Stafford. She claimed to be the daughter of a Louisville judge—except that particular judge didn't have a daughter. This lovely lady attended a lavish ball where she danced all night. She eventually danced herself to death, collapsing onto the ballroom floor, much to the dismay of her partner. She was buried in an unknown grave on the Graham Springs property. However, this may not be the exact story.

Years after this death, the "beautiful girl who danced herself to death in Dr. Graham's ballroom" may not be a mystery after all. There has been speculation of a fiery young lady named Mollie Black of Tazewell, Tennessee, who was the second (and very unhappy) wife of actor Joe Sewell. The actor spent most of his time away from home "satisfying his wanderlust." Unfortunately, being a stay-at-home wife was not what Miss Black wanted. She loved to attend parties and dances, and she often "ran away from her young son and a bickering mother-in-law to enjoy a fling at the rollicking

Kentucky watering place in Harrodsburg." At Graham Springs, she could dance as wildly as she wanted, "forgetting her troubles back in Tennessee."[59]

On the night in question, Mollie Black dashed from one fast dance set after another, rotating between all the eligible dance partners. It was after the last dance of the evening, near midnight, that she fell dead on the floor. Because she registered under a false name and it could not be proved who she checked in with, her body was buried on the grounds of the hotel. A stone marker was placed, and there is currently a sign bearing the words "Unknown. Hallowed and Hushed be the place of the dead. Step Softly. Bow Head."

Like a pressed flower found in a romantic young girl's scrapbook, Mollie Black's headstone represents the "lavender and lace of the ante-bellum South." At one time, the springs of Kentucky were sanctuaries of safety where southerners fled to escape the city haze, which they believed bred malaria and yellow fever. Graham Springs "was a place where no infectious atmosphere sapped the human system of its virility." The "Lone Grave" is a spot of general historic interest in Graham Springs park, and through cooperation of the Woman's Club and City Manager William Gregory, it was suitably marked. A marker was placed beside the sarcophagus some years ago by the club, but time destroyed it and then there was nothing left to tell the story of the beautiful, mysteriously lady whose name was never known. The grave has since been enclosed with a white picket fence and a new permanent sign with the original message.[60]

It is still unknown who this mysteriously lady really was. As we approach the 250th anniversary of Harrodsburg, there has been renewed interest in conducting an archaeology dig on this site to exhume the bones and possibly test for DNA. This is a subject of heated debate in the community—one side wants to leave the grave alone and the other wants to learn the identity of the woman and then properly inter her remains. Only time will tell.

Health Trip to the Tropics

Willis Letter no. 22

Following is a group of letters written by Nathaniel Parker Willis to his friend Morris when Willis stayed at Graham Springs in 1852. They are collected in an out-of-print book called *Health Trips to the Tropics*. Four of the letters are reprinted here so the reader can understand the grandeur of this historic resort and the entrepreneurism of Dr. Graham. The terms "Harrodsburg Springs" and "Graham Springs" are used interchangeably throughout the letters. The letters are reprinted as is from the original publication.

> *Dear Morris,*
>
> *Cincinnati has "sidled-up," as you know, to within 48 hours of New York, and by this same scarcely noticed but perpetual "sidling-up"—(on grease and smooth iron)—the place I write from is likely to become the* central Saratoga *of America. With next year's completion of a railroad now in progress, it will be a couple of hours south from Cincinnati, and then, between New York and New Orleans, Washington and St. Louis, Harrodsburg Springs will be the hub of the wheel of fashion—nearly equip-accessible from these four outside points, and a rallying spot for all the beauty and be-socialness between. Its chief attraction, for Boston, will be, that the summer commences there a month earlier—for New Orleans, that it commences a month later—and in that compromise month of June (shivering at Boston, sultry at New Orleans, but summery to Harrodsburg), it is likely to attract, from North and South, all, at least, who are susceptible to climate. At present the crowded season is in July and August; and, during those months, it is the grand field of tournament for Western flirtation, and the gathering point for politicians out of harness, and for such wealthy Westerners and Southerners as like to spend their money on the side of the Alleghenies that slopes towards home.*
>
> *People and places are so over-trumpeted, now days, that, when we meet with man, woman, or watering place to which common report has not done justice, we feel a kind of compensatory eagerness to make it up to them. I went to Harrodsburg Springs as the best place I could hear of, for a fortnight's loitering—the Northern summer not being ready for my lungs, and Kentucky having some inviting features and qualities of which I wished to see more—but, in the establishment of "The Springs" I expected to find little except clap boards and whitewash, solitude and sanguine expectations of company, a ballroom full of cobwebs, and a vehement negro to ring the bell for meals. I hoped it was such a place, for the loneliness I wanted, and the leisure it would give me to write up my notes of travel. There are hundreds of such places that are more puffed and talked of than is Harrodsburg, with all its real advantages.*
>
> *After a most lovely drive of thirty miles from Lexington, I was landed at a massive gateway of granite, between a couple of bronze lions; and, through the gentle ascending grounds of a courtyard, laid out and shaded*

with exquisite taste, I saw a structure of unusual magnificence, looking every way solid and beautifully finished. Two long wings of cottage buildings enclosed the front court, but the well laid walks seemed to lead off to grounds beyond; and, to enjoy the twilight, I gave my baggage to the servant and started for a stroll before going to my room. I found that the hotel was surrounded by what might well be a nobleman's park, the walks apparently endless and yet carefully and meticulously kept, and the natural advantages of the undulating woodlands charmingly understood and improved. I rambled till the stars came out to light me back to supper, and returned, feeling that I had stumbled upon a most unexpected mixture of paradise and public house.

My private letters have told you with what pleasure, and with what profit to health, I passed two or three weeks at this lovely and luxurious sojourn. Some facts which should be more generally known, with regard to it, I will copy (in a mote) from printed documents, and on the subject—but, before turning to my more personal befalling's, let me speak admiringly of the mere hotel. It is furnished and kept like the best establishments in cities. You could be nowhere more luxuriously comfortable. The wealthy Western families whose equipages daily throng and enliven the gateway, and who take rooms and reside here for months together, with a reference to the fashionable season, are the best evidence of the quality of the accommodations. Good tables, and a good society, are two luxuries which I believe you may always make sure of at Harrodsburg.

But I wish to introduce you to Dr. Graham, the proprietor of this vast establishment. The Doctor is not an individual. And, our language, by the way, is deficient in the phrase which should express what he is, more than an individual. We want something which should correspond to the distinctions we make, for instance, in speaking of land. We say, "a lot," "a farm," "a tract," "a township," "a county"—but, though Dr. Graham is at least a township, if not a county, as to extent of influence and amount of value in the neighborhood, there is no way of denominating him as more than "a lot." To say he is an enterprising and gentlemanly man, does not express a quarter of an acre of the whole county he is. With the ten thousand words said to be in common use, it seems a pity that we should have no means of expressing the graduated magnitude of so varying a thing as a citizen where a single individual amounts to an institution, as Dr. Graham does—or is quite equals, as he is to a quorum, or a committee, or a majority—we should be able to express it by something shorter than writing his biography. I hereby put in my pleas for the amendment to our language.

You would be likely to draw an erroneous conclusion as to the Doctor's character, from the habits of his horse. Of all the gentlemen in the county he is probably the most prompt, expeditious and energetic man of business—yet his horse (which he lent me for a ride every day) walked me straight up to every carriage and horseman on the road, and, spite of whip and other remonstrance, can to a dead halt, and stayed there, till he had heard some conversation. It was occasionally a little embarrassing to me, for, where there were ladies in the carriage, the possible habits of the horse were not likely to occur to them; and, for a stranger to stop them in the middle of the road, and have nothing to say, looked like rather a thinly covered indulgence of curiosity. But the Doctor, though he has time and politeness for everybody (as this confirmed habit of his tall bay horse undeniably betrays), is still of a most omnipresent where he's wontedness. No guest comes or departs without the courteous host's welcome or farewell. No beau's boots have had their chalked bottoms misread, and then left at the wrong door, without an instant meeting between the protruded head of inquiry and the rectifying master of the house. No invalid longs to tell how he has passed the night, without finding the kindest of listeners in the Doctor; and no young lady walks alone on the portico without the Doctor's large Spanish eyes ready at half a glance to come and unload her heart of its eloquent inexplicableness. The innumerable things attended to, for the guest's comfort, and the quantity of time, chat, and personal presence to spare, on the part of the handsome man who does it all, was the miracle of my daily perplexity while at Harrodsburg. But you see from this, what sort of house and host you may find, should you go that far southward to anticipate a June.

And the spirit of the age was not likely to be unwatched by the vigilant eye of Dr. Graham. With his experience as surgeon in the army and practicing physician, he knows the value of health in a world of care and contention; and the general pursuit of it, in connection with pleasure, opened his eyes to the movements of the day—the general Siamese between hydropathy and watering place. Few belles have papas and mammas of undamaged constitutions. Few flaunt in place in the evening, which would not be fairer as well as healthier for a "pack in a set sheet" in the morning. Those who have made a fortune usually have sore need of renovating juices to enjoy it. The summer demand for health and pleasure will so combine the family inclinations as to bring old and young to the same place, if that place furnishes facilities for both. A ballroom, a water-cure establishment, and a good table are the three supplies to combine, for a world that employs its summer solstice to flirt, freshen and fatten.

The hydropathic establishment which has been added to the costly hotel at Harrodsburg, is probably as complete and well-arranged as anyone in the country. No pains and expense have been spared upon it. Dr. Graham came to New York, and after much inquiry, selected Dr. Houghton (whose Lectures on Hydropathy are so well known), as the best medical man who could best found the system of Hydropathy in the West. This gentleman has the present charge of the establishment at Harrodsburg. I was a fortnight under the treatment, while there, and may perhaps write of it, when my experience shall give me more authority to pronounce upon my present impressions. In Houghton's skill and knowledge of the subject, I have unlimited confidence. To a thorough medical education he adds a characteristic carefulness and patience of analysis, and these advantages, with the manners and habits of a most refined gentleman, form desirable hands for an invalid to fall into. I feel incredibly grateful to him. All will, who come under his kind and intelligent care.

Of the town of Harrodsburg itself I have said nothing. It has about two thousand inhabitants, a neighborhood of wealthy proprietors, lots of livery stables and "dry goods" stores, several Female Academics, and (a superfluity for you and me, my dear General, as we are not in politics) Salt River only one mile off! Yes, I rode "up Salt River" every day—and a charming stream with a green bank through the woodlands, that celebrated refuge of disappointment turns out to be. It rises near here and empties into the Ohio just below Louisville. In the quantities of mint that crush under the horse's feet as he follows its windings, I could smell nothing prophetic of the party it is preparing to welcome from the coming campaign.

Things dull in themselves are sometimes valuable for what they suggest. My letter has been written with a brain somewhat out of condition, but if you know more of Harrodsburg Springs by read it, its dullness may well be pardoned.

Yours, Nathan

Willis Letter no. 23

Dear Morris,

It reminded me of you—for it was like falling in with one of the vertebrae of Broadway—to find an omnibus at the door of my Kentucky hotel. I had been reading of the fossil remains of Mammoth Cave, and my first thought was that of stumbling unexpectedly on an organic specimen of

New York or "the General"—antiquities both, to me, so long seemed the four months since I had seen them. The omnibus was doing duty as a stagecoach and was to take me 30 miles to Harrodsburg. How so citified a thing had followed the setting sun so far over the horizon, I could not conjecture; but with four horses, and the baggage on top it bowled merrily away, and worked as well, I thought, as if picking up ladies in Broadway. The sixpence hole, by the way, was not in operation, and should have been stuffed with straw, for it let in the dust uncomfortably.

My traveling companions were five—four men and a gamecock. The latter was sewed up in a pocket handkerchief, and with only his head out, was treated ignominiously as a bundle. I inquired into his history as he rolled about on the floor and on hearing that he had been the victor at the Lexington races, the day before, killing three successive antagonists, and winning considerable money for his master, I could not but philosophize on what may follow glory, in the experiences of heroes. Here was a warrior, with the blood of battle still unwashed from his crest, and who, as Hoffman says of the men of Churubusco, "Was equal in the deeds he wrought, to any common five," tied up in the retirement of a pocket handkerchief and trying in vain to find a support and hold his head up. The ingratitude of this world's fought for! I made some inquiries as to the education and diet of the brave bird—overcoming, meanwhile, considerable disgust at his mater's brutal way of kicking him about the floor of the omnibus; and as it may be useful to know how to get ready for glory, and I will record the process. The Irishman who owned the gamecock, and made a business of it, gave me all the dietetics in a single sentence: "For three weeks afore the fight, feed the feller on egg, cornmeal, rock candy and barley water." In case of an invasion from the Lobos Islands, my dear General, you may be called on to fight for glory and guano, and the recipe may be worth sticking under your belt.

My other omnibus companions were free and kindly. Conversation was unembarrassed. The best dressed man of the three pulled a horn comb from his pocket, after a while, combed his own head and then passed around the utensil. All accepted and made use of it till it came in turn to me, and (not to give offence) I apologized for declining it, on the ground of having a curly heat that took care of itself. The comb-lender was a hater of the men who "owned such a bloody quantity of land, a poor man couldn't get a place to call his own." He pointed to a porter's lodge on one of the beautiful woodland estates we were passing (the road for 30 miles, by the way, seeming to pass through a lordly English park), and said he liked to see a shanty with a pig trough at the door, and fences around small lots—not such a sign as that, of a man's gobbling up more than his share. As to the old Kentuck that God made, belonging to a few of these cussed aristocrats, he didn't believe it was good law. You might as well do without it. Why didn't Cassius Clay take up that idea and not be trying to make gentlemen out of niggers [sic]*?*

Thus, discoursing and exchanging knowledge, we arrived at Kentucky River—and with my eyes wide open—for the descent to its banks, through the valley of what is called Indian Creek, was a perfect gem for an artist. The bed of this tributary stream is deep, through precipitous rocks; and the road follows one of the sides of the ravine, on a sort of corkscrew shelf, every inch revealing some new combination of cliff and foliage. There was one graceful point, more particularly, held forward like a lady's foot to a shoemaker's measure, of which I quite longed for a sketch to bring away. The prettiest known foot of the fashionable world having been born in the immediate neighborhood, I ventured to name this projecting instep of the lovely mountain above; and I beg some friendly artist to pencil and bring it along in his portfolio. Governor Adair's estate is within a mile or two, and "Florida's foot" should be the name of the loveliest reminder of his daughter's beauty. The shower of sonnets written to it at Saratoga, 20 years ago, might be still traced in the fertility of Parnassus.

And now, my dear Morris, consider Kentucky River presented formally to your acquaintance and particular attention—a stranger you should see and know more of. Deepen Trenton Falls for one or two hundred feet, smooth its cascades into a river, and extend it for 30 miles—30 miles between perpendicular precipices from 300 to 500 feet high, and only a biscuit toss across at the top—and you have a river of whose remarkable beauty the world is strangely ignorant. At the point where it is crossed by the route to Harrodsburg, the banks though sublime even here, are less lofty than elsewhere. Of another visit to it, at a bolder point, I have some pleasant memoranda, from which I may scribble, in this or another letter—but meantime I must record the loveliness of the crossing at Brooklyn Ferry. This Kentucky Brooklyn consists of one house under the rock, one fine looking and herculean ferryman, who is also postmaster and father of the family that constitutes the population of the place, and one broad bottomed scow, into which the stagecoach is driven, and which is pulled across by one negro, on a rope pulley. In those ten minutes of gliding noiselessly from the base of one cliff to another, the traveler who loves scenery enjoys a feast. That postmaster ferryman looks like a capitally good fellow (let me chronicle), and to go and lodge a week with him and pull up and down stream in a "dug out," would be a delightful thing for an artist to do—a thing I have put down among my own life's many little reluctant foregoneness. Some idler man will perhaps thank me for this turning down of a leaf of travel for his notice.

A village of shakers lies a few miles beyond Kentucky River, and it is curious to see the effect of celibacy on barns and fences. Things look too virtuous for comfort. I never saw such excessive neatness. The stones of the walls looked as exemplary as if everyone had been catechized and wiped clean with the corner of an apron. Nature had been permitted to retain no more beauty than the laws of fertility made inevitable. The rich apple trees looked sorry they were such sinners as to be beautiful. The green grass seemed rebuked and overawed. A dozen large stone houses were severely well built, and the eight or ten women, whom we saw going to and from, turned in their toes and elbows as if carefully taught to be ungraceful. I walked to an enclosed well for a drink of water, while the broad brimmed postmaster overhauled the mails; and found I was within the fence of Elder Bryant, the head man of the community. It was Saturday evening, and he was at the open window, shaving himself for Sunday—the morrow's law of rest to which the incorrigible beard pays no attention, being enforced upon the more manageable soap and razor. Though in his shirt sleeves and with a face half covered with lather, the Elder had a noble and commanding presence. How so intellectual and dignified a man could ever dance with the women, to worship God—and believe in it—was hard to realize. But he looks sincere and good.

One cannot but admire the operation of the tenets of this sect, as to business matters. Though, by their creed, babies are iniquitous, and the world ought to come to an end, they raise better vegetables and breed better cattle for the support of the present offspring of sin than any other class of farmers. I am assured that every article of produce from the Shaker village brings a third more of price than any other in the markets of the surrounding towns. They prosper. They add yearly to their stock, and their land. What is the secret? Is it in the community principle as to property, and the abstinent principle as to person? Is it in employing the women in the raising of crops instead of the raising of children—reducing them to the level of the men as laborers in the field as well as sharers of the profits? It is that taste, grace, and pleasure are impoverishing principles, and that thrift and beauty cannot, in this fallen world, dwell together? Or, has the awkward dancing or "trying celibacy" nothing to do with it, and is it merely that the world is too largely constructed for any "one-horse concern," and it is against the natural order of things for an individual to be sole proprietor of anything? Who will tell us how we can borrow Shaker prosperity and leave Shaker ugliness's behind? The hominy of human happiness is so hard to separate from the corn's cob and kernel skin!

After such a sermon, this seems a good place for an Amen—so

Yours, etc., Nathan

Willis Letter no. 25

Dear Morris,

I have had a day's experience of crossroad knowledge in the heart of Kentucky, and perhaps, though less imposing than turnpike knowledge, it may interest you to read of its humbler and more homely befalling's. As we may have, here and there, a subscriber to The Home Journal, *who wants but little to wonder at, at a time, an uneventful letter may be excusable, even to publish.*

My hospitable host, Dr. Graham, had been the historian of a curiosity which is almost inaccessible, on the Kentucky River; and a trip to this—twenty miles across the country from Harrodsburg—was the excursion of the day. With an active little horse in a buggy wagon, we were on the road at the hour which the birds make so industrious and musical, our breakfast in its place, and our dinner waiting its turn in a basket. The Doctor was the driver.

And let me record here, by the way, a simple bit of observation which had never occurred to me before—that driving is an art not learned in one generation. If roads were introduced into the Deserts of the East, it would be the Arab's grandchild, not the Arab nor the Arab's son, who might learn to be "a whip." The sequence of wheels after hoofs, and the relative responsibilities of the ears that proceed and the axletree that follows confiding after are secrets no more learned in a day than the scent of game by a race of quadrupeds. The Kentuckian, therefore, who might compete with the Arab sheikh, as the world's best horseman, is no driver. Roads are entirely too new to him. Even at this day, the commonest sight on turnpikes where wheels might be used, is a woman on horseback with three children—the baby in her lap and two urchins astraddle behind to go five or six miles to take tea, most Kentucky mothers, at the present moment, would prefer the saddle. By birth and education, it is consequently a horseback state—the animal at the end of a long pair of reins much too far off for Kentucky instincts of control and comfort.

Entering upon an Archipelago of stumps and rocks after the first mile, I very soon received the impression which I have just recorded. My friend the Doctor—famous when surgeon in the army not whipping off a leg with dexterity, and famous since as the best rifle shot in his neighborhood, had no eye for the liabilities of wheels. He evidently bought a stump done with if the horst went clear of it. It was a wonder, to him, how the buggy came to a standstill upon an obstacle he had thought comfortably left behind. An eloquent man and warm on history and scenery as he rode along, his arms were busy with gestures, and the reins loose about the horse's heels, no matter what the apparent impossibilities or impending antagonisms of the road. The books speak of earthquakes as formerly as frequent in Kentucky that every family had a key suspended over the Bible on the mantel piece, to know by its vibrations when to fall on their knees and pray. The Doctor's driving seemed historically accordant with this—a series of earthquakes, every shock bringing us to our knees—though, as there will be progress with even the worst of iteration, we arrived thus at the precipice overhanging "Dick's River." And here was scenery worth some rough using to get a sight of.

Those who "go to mill" at "Kin's Mills" must seem to have their grain ground on the earth's axle, for the bed of Dick's [Dix] *River, which turns the wheel, is three hundred feet down between almost perpendicular rocks; no complete daylight known there I should suppose, except at high noon. We should properly have been let down by a string but the breeching proved faithful, and we reached the bank of the river, horse first, without being precipitated over the head of the animal most of the way on end At the small bridge spanning the stream sat a man in a picturesque red waistcoat, fishing; and I was struck with the fact, that, though strangers must be comparatively rare in so remote a spot, he never took his eyes from his line to look at us. We crossed the bridge, and, as we went crashing over the loose rocks on the other side, he called out, "They take toll here!" The Doctor pulled up. "Brilliant home," he continued, still keeping his eyes dreamily on the water, and speaking in a tone as low and unexcited as the murmur of the stream, "but I'll take it for him." "Who much?" "Why, they ask a quarter, but I'll make twenty cents answer!" And with this kindly dialogue my friend walked to the contemplative angler and dropped the money into his hand without disturbing the possibility of a coincident nibble. To one surfeited with the "digito monstrari" this might be a pleasant variety of human notice, though the chances were that the traveler, thus made second to some trout, might think himself indifferently treated.*

The village, a few rods up the stream, consisted of the mill and a blacksmith's shop, and here we stopped to inquire our way to the Devil's Pulpit. "I've heard a heap of talk about that place," said the brawny Vulcan, "but I never was thar. Do you know, Jem?" he asked turning to the man wielding the other hammer. But Jem had also lived close to the remarkable spot without going to it, and we took the road slanting up the opposite precipice of the ravine, trusting to the Doctor's reminiscences of a way he had once travelled before.

The tree, in a country that has never been "cut over," are wonderfully majestic, and even the dislocating roughness of the road did not prevent my continual amazement at the beauty of single trees, standing on the green floor of the forest, each one a monarch in mere glory of presence. On the Hudson, so perpetually felled and burned over, you never realize the splendor of the primitive wilderness; and, indeed, it takes all the majesty of the Highlands and Catskills, and all the artificial wonders of steamers and rail trains, to compensate for this comparative nakedness of your beautiful river.

It was in the midst of one of these lofty "mille colonnes" of nature that we came to a log schoolhouse built upon a knoll, and here the Doctor pulled up for another inquiry. The schoolmaster was likely to know where the Devil's Pulpit might stand, and I was interested to see the schoolmaster and his urchins For my visit here, however, and the remainder of my excursion, I shall require the space of another letter I believe, and for the present, adieu.

Willis Letter no. 26

Dear Morris,

The log schoolhouse (at the door of which I left you in my last letter) was so remote from the world, there in the heart of the wilderness, that the laborious acquiring skill in such encounters as ciphering and oratory seemed like the harnessing of knights for a crusade far away. Considering the road we had come over, the arrival of any of these barefooted urchins at the world's battlefields of humbug and cheating seemed too improbable for this trouble of preparing the weapons To recognize the beauty of a tree, and listen to the "still small voices" of conscience and indigestion, would have seemed to me (had I been consulted at the door and had schools been a new invention) the learning for which the necessity was more immediate—though in thickly settled neighborhoods, of course soft sodder and calculation obviously came first.

I wanted Darley at my elbow to sketch the interior of this school. Unconsciousness makes beautiful pictures—the rudeness and grotesqueness of real-life groupings rather adding than otherwise to their effect. While three or four of the larger girls, just entering upon awkward-hood, had their heads on the benches and sat with their chins on their knees, feeling of their toes, there were two or three of the younger ones with grace and beauty enough to equip angels—the heaven they were leaving behind them still radiant in their delicious little faces. Almost as often as I see young children, I quote Woodsworth's beautiful imagining:

"Our birth is but a sleep and a forgetting.
The soul that rises with us, our life's star,
Hath had elsewhere its setting,
And cometh from afar.
Not in entire forgetfulness,
And Not in utter nakedness,
But trailing clouds of glory do we come
From God who is our home."

One I could have taken to my bosom with a hug, and stolen—(to adopt and add to the "Orion's belt of three" who form my constellation at home)—a little fairy, laying flat on her stomach upon the top of a sloping desk, and with her heels in the air and her cheek on her hand, too busy with her spelling book to notice our coming in. Her heaps of curls were masses of brown tanned lighter at the curves, and the russet red of her cheek was beaming with tranquil health—eyes large and steady, hands plumb and dirty, shoulders and back bare, and frock ragged. There she lay, learning to spell; and meantime more beautiful than she will be when the lesson is learned; and better worth admiring and loving than when her heels are kept down, and her rags changed to the petticoats of womanhood. How out of time and place come the things we most want, in this world! I am inclined to think Eden is still around us. Its loveliness and happiness are only mislaid, mislabeled, and unrecognized.

Of the troop on the board bench provided for the jacket and trouser department of the school, one-half at least were picking the cay from between the logs, and so getting a look at the open air outside; and they had so far succeeded that the four walls let in the light like a honeycomb. There was one window—a hole sawed through one of the logs, that is to say—but the main supply of daylight that had been calculated for, evidently came through the door Near this stood the tall, erect, majestic form of the schoolmaster—certainly, the largest supply of dignity for the money (twenty-five dollars a month) which I had yet seen in my travels. How so handsome a man could see himself in the glass once a day, and keep that school for the pay, I presume Providence knew and provided—but he seemed to me to have Nature's ticket on his brow for the government of older minds.

To our inquiries for the way to the Devil's Pulpit, the schoolmaster shook his head—but up spoke the biggest boy in the school. He knew where it was—some people called it "Candlestick Rock"—it was two miles off, and he would go and show us the way. And, kindness and cheerfulness, with which this young Kentuckian of sixteen gave us four hours of his time and attention, I should like to have a "seed for planting." Our way was through a wilderness partially cleared, and every quarter of a mile brought us to a gate, or to heaps of just-felled timber, to be navigated with great care by horse and wagon; and with this bright lad for guide and gate-opener, we were "only passengers." He took us to the Devil's Pulpit, and brought us back, walking before or at the side of our wagon, and conversing as fearlessly and unsuspiciously as a nobleman taking his guest over his park. I like the grace and self-confidence of the boy. The highest cultivation of courts and palaces would only take such manners round a circle and bring them back to where they are.

Near the point of our journey we came to a settler's farmhouse, and here we unhitched our active little locomotive, and left him to "wood up" for the passage back Our own basket of provender was here remembered also, though, as we had arrived just at the dinner hour, the hospitable backwoodsman pressed us hard to go in and dine We rather gave offence, I thought, by insisting on sitting down to our own sandwiches and liquids in the outer room—the ladies, whom we should have seen at table, not making their appearance at all—but our host was all kindness, and after looking to our horse, he offered to accompany us in our visit to the point of curiosity.

This Kentucky farm looked like a scene of vigorous industry, though the first beginnings of civilization are very unsightly. Woods are exceptionally beautiful, but half a wood cut down is like a half a house torn away—leaving a front most ruinously un-architectural. Then trees prostrate in all directions, fences of logs and branches stumps just high enough to look aghast, ad nature's rude rocks exposed and dug around by the plough, are dismal features to a landscape. Our friend was very communicative on the way, and gave us, in his own history, a curious type of the American facility for "getting on." When he first came into that part of the country, he had nothing, but the protested five hundred dollars note of a broken merchant. On the possibility of its being eventually paid, he managed to buy four hundred acres of land, of which he now had one hundred and thirty under cultivation. It was a proviso in the purchase that he should give the land back after a certain number of years, if it was not paid for—his labor on the soil, of course, being rent as well as security to the original owner. He had married, owned three negroes, and, by the cattle in all direction, his farm was numerously stocked. He was a broad backed, cheerful, happy looking man. Those who have seen the working population of Europe, know what there is to emigrate for, in such a contrast to their condition as is presented in this picture.

By no paths, but over chasms and rocks so wild, and so seldom visited that the hawks and eagles flew around and over without fear of us, we arrived at the point, in the abysm called Kentucky River, where stands "Candlestick Rock." It is a column which the action of water has separated from the precipice, and left toppling and alone—in shape and form like a pile of muffins, but two hundred feet high. Dr. Graham's description (which I sent you with my last letter) gives you the detailed dimensions of it. It is a wonder, yet it is but part of a wilderness of wonders This strangely deep-down river is here at its finest point of precipitous walling in. A projected railroad is to cross it, at this place, I understand, and when that is completed, they will need a station house on the riverbank, for the traveler will not go by, without stopping to climb about and admire. It is a most beautiful and picturesque state, Kentucky! Give us but facilities for getting into it, and its scenery will be a constant attraction for visitors from the North.

I must abruptly close my letter, my dear Morris.

Chapter 3

THE NEW GRAHAM SPRINGS HOTEL

1911–1932

Graham Springs Hotel...right in the heart of the Bluegrass region, with its tennis, croquet, and shady grounds, is located on a high eminence with splendid views and amid beautiful scenery...is kept in fine condition and its water, as with many other springs in close proximity, is well-known to health-seekers from many parts of the county.

—Courier-Journal, *July 3, 1924*

Cassell Mansion Converted into New Graham Springs Hotel

In 1887, a portion of the old Graham Springs property was auctioned for $19,001 to Edgar H. Gaither. Mr. Gaither represented a Louisville syndicate that, in turn, donated some of the land to the City of Harrodsburg for the development of Youngs Park. One year later, the remaining thirty acres of property, including the Epsom springs, were sold to Kentucky Real Estate and Improvement Association.

In 1888, the property was purchased by Jonathan I. Cassell, chair of the Kentucky Democratic convention at the time. A successful lawyer and prominent Harrodsburg citizen, Cassell decided to build a handsome mansion as a private residence for himself and his family. The residence was a Romanesque-style house, with stone arches and a tower, and was built on a hill where Haggin Memorial Hospital is now located.

—E H. Gaither bought Harrodsburg Springs, the government property, which sold at auction Friday for $19,001 cash. It is reported that the purchase was for a Louisville syndicate.

A newspaper clipping for the sale of a portion of Harrodsburg/Graham Springs from the *Interior Journal*, July 19, 1887. *Author's collection.*

Also on this property was the Mercer County Fair and Horse Show, the oldest continuous fair and horse show in the United States. Dating from 1828, there were several locations for the event in Mercer County, but the present location was purchased from Cassell in 1904 and was once a part of the Harrodsburg/Graham Springs property.

The Cassell family occupied this private home until 1910, when it was sold to Ben Casey Allin, then longtime clerk of the Mercer Circuit Court. After Allin brought the property, he decided to open the spacious house as a hotel for summer boarders who wished to drink from the famed water and breathe pure air. A vast majority of the grounds were in the shade, with the forest trees planted by Graham long ago, drawing the surroundings into a close, intimate feel. Mr. and Mrs. Allin were assisted by Alice Ware, and together they worked to make a new history for Graham Springs.[61]

It is worth noting the old Graham Springs Hotel only has one lithograph drawing to provide visible evidence of its existence. With the start of photography in the 1820s, it would seem like photographs would exist of such a unique resort before the main building burned in the 1850s. However, the new Graham Springs hotel and grounds are well documented. The resort was smaller and more manageable, and the popularity of "taking the waters" was still fashionable and affordable, although times were rapidly changing. After the turn of the century, more guests were coming than Allin could accommodate in the house, so he added rooms to the original mansion, built cottages and constructed a large combination dining room and ballroom. But "a day that is dead will ever come back" proved true, and with the war and Depression, the days of leisure and elegance were over. The last Graham Springs Hotel closed in 1934.[62]

A historical postcard of the New Graham Springs Hotel, circa 1915. *Author's collection.*

A historical postcard of the last spring from Graham Springs, located on Linden Avenue in Young's Park. *Author's collection.*

In August 1910, the *Courier-Journal* ran the following advertisement:

> *Plan to re-establish Graham Springs Resort—*
> *A plan is on foot to open a fine sanitorium here on the site of the once famous Graham Springs Hotel, which, before the war, was considered the finest summer resort in the South and was called "The Saratoga of the South." The water of Graham Springs contains rare medicinal properties. Over half of the capital stock of $50,000 has been subscribed, and it is thought the entire amount will be obtained during the coming week.*

Allin made plans for extensive improvements to Graham Springs Hotel via an expansion of the resort that enlarged the property to accommodate at least fifty more guests. A large dining hall, artesian well, bathrooms and twenty more sleeping apartments were among the improvements.[63]

The following article appeared in a 1911 edition of the *Kentucky Advocate*:

> *It will be pleasant news to the people of Central Kentucky to learn that the far-famed historical old Graham Springs will be opened as a select summer resort the coming season. The Cassell mansion, one of the most elegant brick buildings in the Bluegrass has been converted into a choice hotel. Old fashioned cooking will be provided and food in abundance will be supplied. The water that pours from Old Graham Springs is the finest in the world and it is a wonder that somebody has not long ago erected a hotel there sufficient enough to accommodate five hundred guests. The property is now owned by Mr. Ben C. Allin and editor T. Sanders Orr has charge of the publicity department. The water from these springs should be bottled and shipped throughout the country. Reasonable rates will be made. Many people will doubtless take advantage of the fine accommodations and benefit themselves by drinking the pure water that made Harrodsburg famous sixty years ago.*[64]

By 1913, the Graham Springs Hotel started having an opening celebration and annual ball on the Saturday after Memorial Day. These celebrations and dances attracted visitors from as far away as New York, as well as many local celebrities. During the 1914 season, Allin started offering semi-monthly dances in the ballroom, open to guests at the Hotel as well as other visitors to Harrodsburg.

In 1919, the handle was removed from the pump at the Graham's Saloon Spring pavilion at Youngs Park by order of Mayor Pulliam. This was done at

GRAHAM SPRINGS HOTEL
HARRODSBURG, KY.

18th Annual Opening Dinner and Dance
Friday Evening, May 27, 1927

Chicken and Country Ham Dinners our Specialty
Special Attention to Parties, Receptions
and Affairs of all kinds

Sole owners of the famous Greenville and Graham Springs
Mineral Water

BEN C. ALLIN, Proprietor

A newspaper clipping about the new Graham Springs Hotel from the *Kentucky Advocate*, May 27, 1927. *Author's collection.*

the request of the chairman of the local board of health because a sample of the water had been sent to the experiment station at Lexington. An analysis by bacteriologist E.J. Gott showed the water to be badly contaminated. The spring was cleaned out and the water purified under the direction of an expert from the experiment station. As soon as this was done, the spring was once more opened to the public. The contaminated water did not affect Allin at the Graham Springs Hotel because this water was supplied from another source. By 1920, Allin was busy drilling several new wells on his Graham Springs property.[65]

Ben Allin loved coon hunting, and he prided himself on having the champion coon dog of Central Kentucky. He once said that he believed "his canine's propensity for trailing the coon is not impaired by his association with a young fox."[66] Allin was known to have a pet fox he also kept on the springs property. The dog and Reynard the fox become fast friends and companions and played together all day long. When ex-sheriff John Morgan heard Allin boast that he had the best coon dog in the area, he said, "Just wait until the season opens. I have one that will make your dog look like a counterfeit when it comes to trailing coons." The coon hunting season did not open until October 1, and usual hunts were on the Salt and Chapin Rivers and at Deep Creek. Morgan and Allin, as well as others from Mercer County, awaited with deep interest the opening of the 1920 season and the biggest coon dog contests ever held in this section. Unfortunately, after searching through numerous newspapers from 1920, I was unable to find out the winner of this contest.

November 9–15, 1920, Antonin and Grace Sterba of Chicago held their Art Exhibit and Harp Recital at Graham Springs Hotel. The complementary exhibit was offered to the public. Antonin was an instructor at the Chicago

A historical postcard of a spring on the property of Graham Springs. *Author's collection.*

A historical postcard of the Saloon Spring at Graham Springs. *Author's collection.*

A photograph of coon hunting in Mercer County, circa 1940. *Harrodsburg Historical Society.*

Art Institute and the Chicago Art Academy. He and his talented wife spent their vacation in Harrodsburg, where he made sketches of High Bridge and surrounding sections. This was the couple's first visit to the Bluegrass, and they were flattered by the people of Harrodsburg. Sterba had art exhibits scheduled in Louisville and Lexington, and while his paintings were in Harrodsburg, he decided to accept the invitation of Allin to have them on display at Graham Springs Hotel.

Antonin Sterba was a Bohemian artist, born at Hermanec, Moravia, but came to America as a youth and achieved phenomenal success in portrait painting. He was a gold medal pupil of the Chicago Art Institute and went abroad, studying at the Julien Academy, Paris; he was also a pupil of the great masters Jean Paul Laurents and Benjamin Constant. He was a member of three of the most prominent societies of artists in Chicago.

Grace Sterba was one of the foremost harpists in the United States and was for years at the head of the Harp Department of the Chicago Conservatory of Music. She studied with the noted Edmund Schnecker of Vienna and Alfred Toulane of New York. As a child, she was harpist at Grace Episcopal Church, Chicago, and did concert work with the Theodore Thomas Orchestra. She had done much recital work and was harp soloist at both the Station Federation and the National Federation of Woman's Clubs held in Wisconsin.[67]

Harrodsburg's 150th Anniversary Celebration

A 1923 *Advocate-Messenger* advertisement for the Graham Springs Hotel promoted its "tennis, croquet, and shady grounds, is located on a high eminence with splendid views and amid beautiful scenery." Perhaps this was the first of what today is known as farm-to-table because "its table is supplied with the best of foods, old-fashioned cooking, chicken dinners, including Jersey milk from our own herd, fresh vegetables and fruit from our own gardens."

In preparing for the 150th anniversary celebration of Harrodsburg, a "Pioneer Luncheon" was served at the Graham Springs Hotel on June 16, 1923, with some two hundred guests being present and a unique menu arranged for the occasion. The tomato salad was termed "Love Apple Salad," taking its name from the early term for tomatoes; the early potatoes were designated "First Settlers"; the chicken was called "Ann McGinty Fowl," being named for one of the most famous of the women of the time; the iced tea was disguised as "Elixir of 1776"; and the other dishes were named accordingly. Professor M.A. Cassidy of Lexington read Paul Lawrence Dunbar's poem "When the Corn Pone's Hot." Henry Cleveland Wood presided as toastmaster.[68]

A special ceremony at Pioneer Cemetery, Old Fort Hill, was the feature of the morning program before everyone retired to Graham Springs. Following the luncheon and talks, a general discussion was held, and plans for the 150th anniversary celebration in 1924 were outlined.[69]

Harrodsburg celebrated its 150th anniversary on June 16, 1924, with a massive pageant garnering statewide support and drawing attention to the city and its history. Maude Ward Lafferty, a resident of Cynthiana, Kentucky, who served as chairman of the Department of History of the Kentucky Federation of Women's Clubs, wrote the script for the production, which supporters proudly promoted as the first statewide pageant ever attempted in Kentucky.

By incorporating the family stories of individuals who could claim genetic link to members of Harrod's band of settlers, Lafferty authored the script for *Pageant of Kentucky's Historical Past*. She made clear that ancestor worship motivated the fort in an article entitled "Other Times and Other Manners Are Kept Alive in the Cabins in Harrod's Fort." In this piece, published in *Kentucky Progress Magazine* in both 1932 and 1934, Lafferty portrayed life at the fort as stirring and heroic. She particularly celebrated the archetypal pioneer woman, whom she believed was "young and wholesome and comely and quite as courageous as her husband."

Top: A historical postcard of Harrodsburg's 150th anniversary pageant at Graham Springs, June 16, 1924. This one depicts the heroic women of Bryan Station. *Author's collection.*

Bottom: A historical postcard of Harrodsburg's 150th anniversary pageant at Graham Springs, June 16, 1924. This one depicts the marriage of Betsy Calloway at Fort Boonesborough. *Author's collection.*

Celebrating Kentucky's growth since 1774, the pageant presented a story of progress in which Americans of European descent tamed a savage wilderness and forged the territory into a state. Twenty-seven of the state's counties participated in this celebration, which drew on club members and university faculty from across the state. Costing $30,000 to stage, the performance was presented in Graham Springs Park, a facility featuring more unobstructed space than Old Fort Hill.

Other Activities at the New Graham Springs

In 1924, a large number of local young people, under the chaperonage of Mrs. Jennie C. Grubbs, county demonstration agent for Boyle County, enjoyed themselves immensely for the week at Graham Springs. The annual encampment of the Poultry and Canning Clubs had a number of speakers of note in attendance to address the members on subjects of an interesting and instructive nature, and the occasion proved to be a most delightful one for all who are fortunate enough to be present.[70]

A Colonial dinner for the Sons of Colonial Wars and the Colonial Dames was held at Graham Springs Hotel on June 16, 1926, in recognition of their joint gift of a handsome gateway at the main entrance of the Pioneer State Park. This gift was made on the 152nd anniversary of the founding of Harrodsburg, the only colonial town in Kentucky.[71]

In 1927, about fifty fox hunters of Mercer County met at the Graham Springs Hotel and made plans for the organization of the Mercer County Fox Hunters' Association. The purpose of the organization was to help officials enforce the dog laws, to protect the sheep and to protect dog owners who obey the dog laws. A committee was appointed to draft by-laws for a permanent organization, and the laws were presented for approval at the next meeting. Members of the committee were Judge Ben C. Allin, Howard Forsythe and Wayne Watts.[72]

Judge Ben Casey Allin announced a run for the Democratic nomination for Congress in 1928. As the county judge of Mercer and the owner of Graham Springs, he was a man of many business affairs. He was circuit clerk for a number of years and had a large following in Mercer and adjoining counties; however, Allin was defeated in the attempt for the nomination.[73]

In addition to patients visiting Graham Springs for health reasons, the ballroom and meeting rooms were used for many purposes, including reunions, graduations, birthday and anniversary celebrations and dances.

A historical postcard of the impressive gate at Old Fort Harrod State Park. *Author's collection.*

A historical postcard of the new Graham Springs Hotel, circa 1915. *Author's collection.*

Local newspapers of the time were full of Mr. or Mrs. So and So returning home after a visit to Graham Springs or Mr. So and So hosting an extravagant party at Graham Springs. In addition to local residents who took part activities, some of the following also help regular meetings and luncheons:

- Local Ruritan, Kiwanis, VFW, Masons and Men's and Women's Clubs
- Central Kentucky Retail Merchants' Association
- Junior Agricultural Clubs of Mercer and Boyle Counties providing weeklong camps for young boys
- Morgan Men Association
- Lexington Country Club

An interesting story appeared in the *Advocate-Messenger* in 1929. Realizing that daybreak was hardly a time for a tourist to visit the Pioneer Memorial State Park, hostesses at the park were puzzled when they found a shivering youth huddled at the gate as the sun came up. They took him into the fort and gave him food and drink before he finally told his story. He was a freshman from the University of Kentucky and an initiate to a fraternity. His

A historical postcard of the Graham Springs pavilion at the Saloon Spring. *Author's collection.*

particular instructions were to get a quart of water from old Graham Springs and then make a drawing of the fort. After resting as the guest of the park hostesses, the weary freshman started his long journey back to Lexington, carrying a jug of mineral water and a map of the fort.[74]

Graham Springs Hotel Is Sold

The famous Graham Springs and new Graham Springs Hotel were sold at a Master Commissioner's Sale for $16,500 in September 1932. Glave and Annie Bell Goddard of Beaumont Inn were the purchasers. The property was sold to satisfy a debt of $15,000. Goddard, who was successful in the management of Beaumont Inn, building it rapidly into popularity and prominence, announced that he would continue to operate the Graham Springs Hotel in connection with Beaumont.[75]

By May 1933, improvements at Graham Springs Hotel were nearing completion, and the hotel was about ready to open as an annex for the overflow from Beaumont Inn. Goddard and Thomas Curry Dedman Jr. were to manage the hotel, but Goddard died just before the renovations were complete.[76]

The Graham Springs resort property—consisting of a hotel, mineral springs and thirty acres of land—was sold by Annie Bell Goddard in May 1935. The owner of Beaumont Inn sold the property to Mineral Springs Products Company Inc. at an unannounced price.[77]

For many years, scientists and research workers sought the secret of liquefying sulfur for the treatment of arthritis, neuritis and other ailments, and thousands of dollars have been expended in the search. Graham Springs was the only institution in the country pioneering these types of treatments. In 1936, the new owners developed a process known only to them: water-soluble liquid sulfur. William A. Caudill, the president of the Mineral Springs Products, spent a number of years perfecting the discovery of liquid sulfur at Graham Springs. It was supported by more than thirty-five physicians over the state of Kentucky, including Dr. E.M. Howard, president of the Kentucky State Board of Health.

Via bath treatment, thermostatically controlled water saturated with liquid sulfur was used in handling case of all forms of skin diseases. Glass-lined tubs, of standard model and of Roman type, the only ones of their kind in America, were used, and each treatment table had an ultraviolet ray light. Two large rooms containing six baths and four treatment tables each

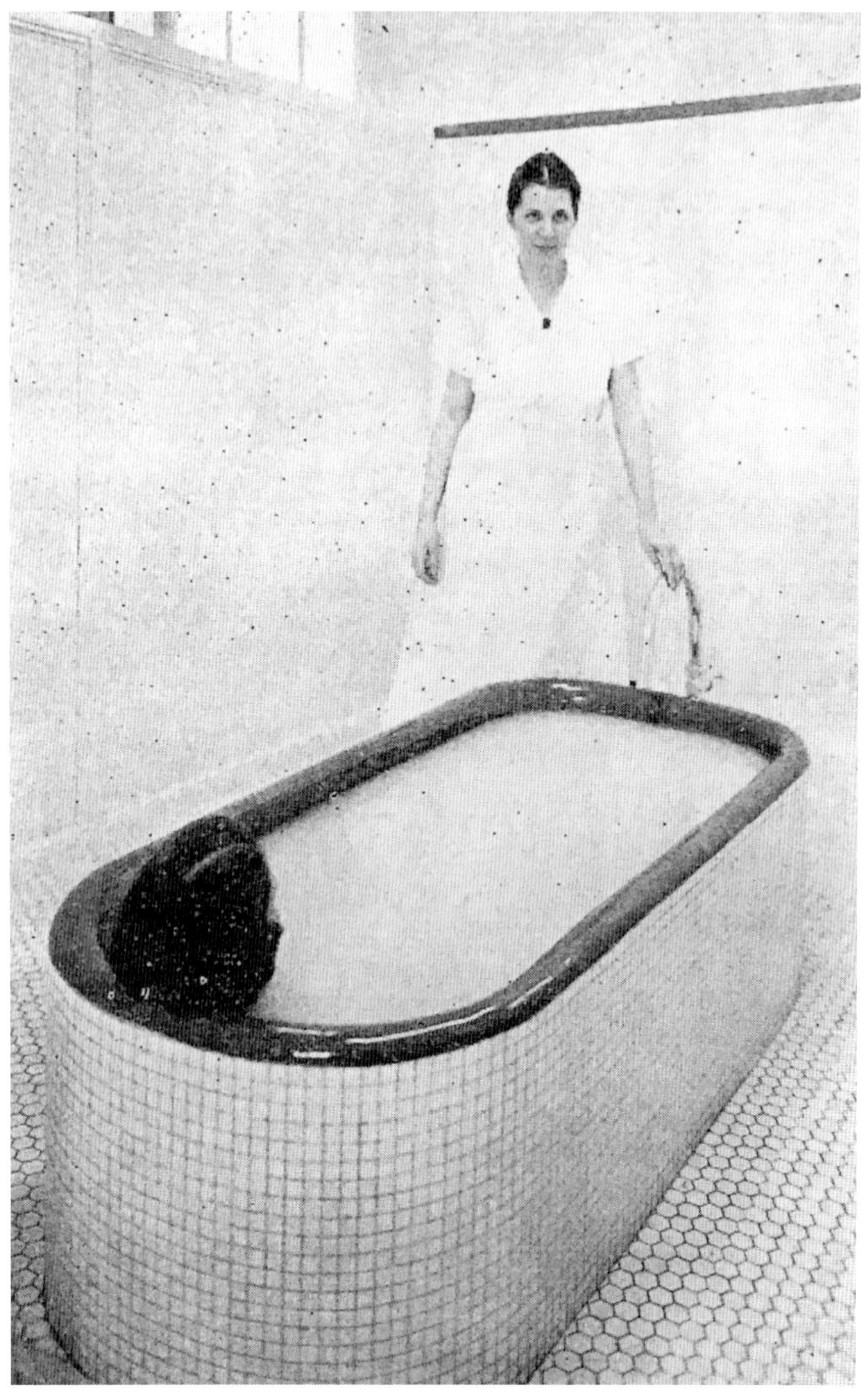

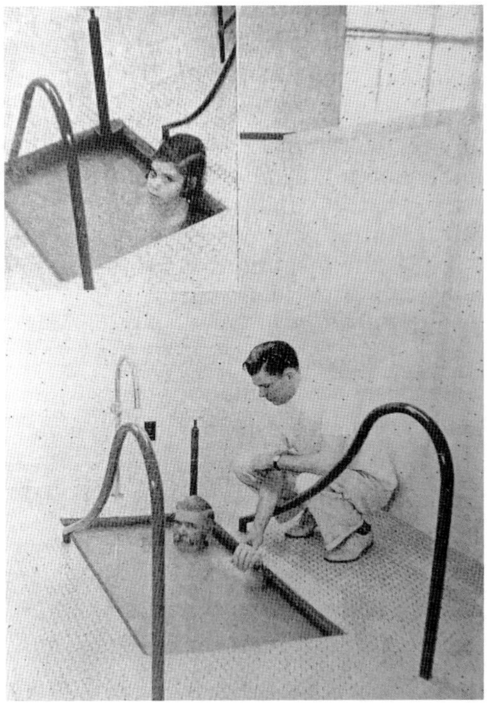

Opposite: A photograph from a historical pamphlet of the above-ground spa tub at the new Graham Springs Resort. *Author's collection.*

Right: A photograph from a historical pamphlet of the in-ground spa tubs at the new Graham Springs Resort. *Author's collection.*

Below: A newspaper clipping of the new Graham Springs Resort from the *Lexington Herald-Leader*, June 12, 1926. *Author's collection.*

GRAHAM SPRINGS

An Ethical Institution with Modern Equipment

for the treatment of
Arthritis, Neuritis, Rheumatism, Sciatica, High Blood Pressure.
Skin Diseases
Stomach, Liver, Kidney and Kindred Disorders.

Graham Springs Has the Most Modern Bath House in America.

Situated in the Cradle of the Commonwealth of Kentucky.

GRAHAM SPRINGS
HARRODSBURG, KENTUCKY
Dr. R. T. Ballard, Physician in Charge
Graham Springs "The Saratoga of the South" is given recognition in the United States Dispensatory.

were included in the sulfur-hydrotherapy department and were kept clean and sanitary at all times.

The Graham Springs water was recognized in the U.S. Dispensatory, and the only liquid sulfur in existence at the time was used there. The complex had a complete staff of nurses and masseuses, as well as complete diagnostic equipment, including X-ray and fluoroscope, under the direction of Dr. Ralph T. Ballard, physician in charge, and Dr. A.B. Patterson, his assistant.

In June 1937, concentrated colloidal sulfur from Graham Springs was being used by state and local experts in an interesting experiment in the control of coccidiosis in chicks. At this period in history, the disease was killing millions of chicks every year, and its control would mean a huge savings to poultry raisers. Unofficial tests of the concentrated mineral water showed surprising results, and the outcome of official tests was awaited eagerly by those in charge, according to Mercer Extension agent C.F. Park.

The official tests were conducted under the direction of Dr. W. Dimock, head of the Kentucky Department of Animal Pathology at the experiment station, and supervised by Park, Stanley Canton (field agent in poultry from the experiment station) and Dr. Ballard. The demonstration set up by Caton, Park and Ballard consisted of chicks selected from a Mercer County flock that tests showed were afflicted with the coccidiosis organism. The chicks were divided into lots and placed in two categories—one as a control group and the other for treatment with the sulfur concentrate. Forty baby chicks free from disease were taken to the experiment station by Dr. Ballard. They were infected with coccidiosis germs by Dr. Dimock and his staff. Four pens of ten chicks each were used for the experiment, with one additional pen of ten disease-free chicks.[78]

In July 1938, Dr. Ballard resigned from his position at the Graham Springs sanitarium, and Dr. F. Becker became the physician in charge. During the summer of 1938, Dr. Becker, speaking for the Graham Springs Company, formally offered the board of city commissioners the proposition to have the city take over one hundred acres of Graham Springs land for a municipal golf course and city recreation center. Mayor Errol Draffen expressed approval of the plan if arrangements could be worked out to the satisfaction of both parties. A motion was adopted by the board favoring the acceptance of the offer if such a plan can be adopted. The mayor said that the city probably could get Works Progress Administration (WPA) aid in improving the land. A meeting was called to discuss details of the plan, but history proved that this idea never got past the planning stage.[79]

Two of Kentucky's most popular products at the time—foxhounds and fine horses—added greatly to the success of the 1939 program of the 106-year-old Mercer County Fair and Horse Show. Hundreds of sleek hounds bayed continuously from their positions on the platform at the bench show, which was held in a wooded dell in the Graham Springs park adjoining the fairgrounds.

Drawn here through their interest in foxhound competitions, members of the board of directors of the National Foxhounds Association held their annual business meeting and dinner at Avalon Inn on Main Street, Harrodsburg, with ten states represented. In connection with the foxhound bench show, hunters and jumpers were judged on the half-mile track at the Mercer Fairgrounds in the twenty-acre Lake field adjoining the grandstand on the south, a tract recently acquired by the fair association for this purpose.[80]

The Saloon Spring, located on Linden Avenue, was one of the most noted of the several mineral water sources that made Graham Springs famous. Many local residents drank the water, claiming it had health-giving qualities, and some even said that they would rather drink it polluted than not at all. However, water at the Saloon Spring was a long source of worry for the Harrodsburg Board of Commissioners, and it was closed in November 1940 by order of the county health officer, Dr. E.C. Humphrey.

A historical postcard of the Saloon Spring at Graham Springs, showing the dirt road. *Author's collection.*

The commissioners were besieged by former users of the water, asking the city to reopen the spring. Several citizens of Harrodsburg, including Mayor Draffen, called attention to an article appearing in the *Harrodsburg Herald* in 1941, "Mineral Spring at Harrodsburg Popular Despite Pollution; Search for Pure Sources Started." Although this suggested bad water at Graham Springs, it actually referred to the Saloon Spring, a spring in Young's Park, which adjoins the Graham Springs sanitarium property. The water on the Graham Springs property was drawn from wells more than two hundred feet deep and was absolutely pure.[81]

Probing for the source of water contamination at the Saloon Spring started on June 20, 1941, in an effort to determine the reason for the pollution. Investigation into the spring was conducted under the management of Mayor Draffen and a committee, including City Manager E.H. Davis and Commissioners Tom Squifflett and Maurice Watts. However, the source of the contamination was not found, and the water of the Saloon Spring on Linden Avenue was permanently shut off.

Graham Springs Property Sold for Community Hospital

After many incarnations, in October 1945, the historic Graham Springs property was purchased by the board of directors at the A.D. Price Memorial Hospital for $40,000. The hospital had accumulated enough money to pay cash for Graham Springs, using an account balance of $11,000 and the proceeds from the sale of the downtown hospital property. The hospital board studied the Graham Springs buildings and decided to add to and remodel the present complex to make it into a modern hospital.[82]

Hospital care started in Harrodsburg as early as 1876 with the "Dr. Smedley house" on South College Street. John Smedley was a successful druggist and physician who saw patients in his home as well as made house calls. In 1914, this grand old brick house was torn down to make way for the construction of the A.D. Price Memorial Hospital, named after Dr. Ansel Daniel Price. The plan for a modern hospital originated with the civic department of the Woman's Club of Harrodsburg and the building of Price Hospital in 1915. This twenty-bed hospital served for thirty-four years until 1945, when a decision was made to build a larger one.[83]

At this point in time, the housing shortage in Harrodsburg was so acute that the board of the A.D. Price Memorial Hospital used the recently purchased Graham Springs property and turned one of the large building into six apartments, to be rented until May 1946, when the planned remodeling was to begin.[84]

In 1946, building lots were offered at auction by Mrs. Henry Cleveland Wood at the Graham Springs addition, property that fronted on Cedar Street. These lots were purchased by the following: Mrs. J. Donald Edwards and son, George Edwards, two lots totaling $1,825; Floyd Hicks and Cecil Brown, two lots for $1,850; E.C. Stephenson, one lot for $975; and Edwin Elliott, one lot for $550. The sale was held by C.E. Rankin, attorney for Mrs. Wood, with Calvin Shewmaker serving as auctioneer.[85]

A goal of $175,000 was set to complete the building of Mercer General Hospital, and $75,400 was donated by Harrodsburg citizens toward this goal. Dr. C.B. VanArsdall Sr., member of the hospital board and chairman of the drive for cash, proclaimed that the building would be completed by January 1, 1949.

The part of the sanitarium containing a large number of bedrooms, which was built when the health resort was enlarged, was retained by the hospital board. The main brick building, which formerly housed the sanitarium, was fireproofed and remodeled, and additional necessary buildings were constructed. The large dining room and kitchen annex of the property were razed, leaving only one wing containing all the modern equipment for the medicinal baths of the sanitorium.[86]

The new hospital was of colonial design, with a pillared portico; it was fireproof throughout. In an emergency, its normal capacity of fifty-two beds could be increased to seventy, and it was two stories with full basement.[87]

Mercer General Hospital Name Changed to James B. Haggin Memorial

The Mercer General Hospital Board of Directors announced that effective January 1, 1954, the name of the hospital would be changed to the James B. Haggin Memorial Hospital. This was to honor the late James B. Haggin, a native of Harrodsburg, whose widow made frequent and liberal gifts to the hospital. Since as early as 1938, Margaret Voorhies Haggin's gifts inspired the board and made possible both the purchase of the grounds and the erection of the modern fifty-two-bed hospital. Since 1942, substantial grants have been made through the Margaret Voorhies Haggin Trust in Memory of James B. Haggin.[88]

The James B. Haggin Memorial Hospital sign currently above the entrance. *Keith Rightmyer.*

After fifty-five years in operation, a fundraising drive started in 2005 to again raise funds for the remodeling of Haggin Hospital. In order to make room for the updated design of the extension and parking area, the huge old oak trees in front of the property, planted by Dr. Graham in the 1840s, were cut down. The original white columns used on the old hospital were incorporated into the new design.

Haggin Hospital Sold to Ephraim McDowell

After more than sixty-eight years in operation, the small community James B. Haggin Memorial Hospital was sold to the larger Ephraim McDowell Regional Medical Center. The name was changed to Ephraim McDowell James B. Haggin Hospital, which recognizes the long legacy of healthcare provided by the two entities.

Chapter 4

OTHER SPRINGS IN HARRODSBURG AND MERCER COUNTY

Salt, available at natural springs, seasonally attracted great herds of bison which through years of repetitious movement carved an extensive system of buffalo traces: avenues used by Anglo-Americans in settling portions of the Ohio Valley.
—John A. Jakle, "Salt on the Ohio Valley Frontier, 1770–1820," Annals of the Association of American Geographers *59, no. 4 (December 1969)*

In Mercer County, there are numerous medicinal springs. They burst out near the summit of the ridges on which the village of Harrodsburg is built. The mass of these ridges is composed of limestone, much of which is of a fine grain, and impregnated with magnesia.

Most of Kentucky's watering places were originally salt licks. The word *lick* was meant literally because "buffalo by the thousands made great roads into [the licks] and licked out deep tranches in the salt-impregnated clay." Some of these trenches were deep enough to conceal a man on horseback as he rode through them. The early hunters, white and Native American, treasured salt licks. The Native Americans unquestionably had known of Kentucky's mineral springs and their curative powers long before the pioneers discovered them. The salt licks also drew the game—some to lick the salt and others to prey on the herbivorous animals at the lick.

Land speculators searched out licks and claimed them whenever possible because salt was essential as a preservative for meat, the staple wilderness diet. The pioneers could no more survive without salt than without weapons and gunpowder. A salt lick considerably enhanced the value of the land on which it was located.

In Kentucky, as Native American warfare faded to a grim memory, towns began growing, the economy strengthened and at last Kentuckians had time and money as well as a long-suppressed urge for entertainment. In an astonishingly short period, these humble salt licks, with their medicinal waters, were transformed into glittering, sophisticated, fashionable spas where the elite and well-to-do came from all over the country to take the waters and have a fabulous time doing it.

The following are other noteworthy, historical springs located in Harrodsburg and Mercer County.

The Big Spring

Amid the chilling winds of March 1774, James Harrod and his company of thirty-one men traveled by canoes from Grave Creek near Wheeling, Virginia, down the Monongahela and Ohio Rivers into the mouth of the Kentucky River. The rivers would have been running swift and high from melting snow and thawing ice. The men should have arrived in central Kentucky by April. The Kentucky River led to the area to become known as Harrod's Landing on Oregon Creek, in the lower end of present-day Mercer County and east of the town of Salvisa. They then came across the Salt River near the area that would become McAfee's Station, up to present-day Fountainbleu Springs and finally to a creek, later to be known as Town Creek. They pushed on up the creek until they came to its source at the Big Spring. It was here where Harrod's company made camp and the eventual settlement of Harrod's Town.[89]

In 1774, Kentucky was part of Virginia and under the Virginia Frontier Settlement Act. If you traveled west across the Appalachian Mountain range to the land that is now Kentucky, you had to designate your claim by cutting your "mark" into the trees at the four corners of your land and live on it one year, or plant a corn crop on it, and then the land was yours. Harrod and his men began laying off a town on June 16, 1774, and they named it Harrod's Town, which became the first permanent English settlement west of the Allegheny Mountains, later to be called Harrodsburg. The men

The Big Spring, where James Harrod and his company landed in 1774—the beginnings of the town of Harrodsburg. *Keith Rightmyer.*

started clearing the roads of Harrod's Town on the south side of Town Creek. These extended a half mile in an east–west direction, where the road originated at a point near the Big Spring Station camp and terminated near the site where the Old Fort would later be erected in 1775–76.[90]

At one point in history, the Big Spring was also referred to as Boiling Springs because the water appeared to "boil from the ground." This should not be confused with the Boiling Springs Station founded by James Harrod, six miles from Harrodsburg. Harrod drew an out-lot in the lottery for land near Harrodsburg, and he found that the site had an abundance of spring water and named his station Boiling Springs.

Though technically not a fort, the area used by settlers in 1774 was where three to five log cabins were built below the Big Spring and enclosed with large "hoop poles" or sapling trees. They were sharpened at the top, and the base was firmly set in a trench that was opened up around the cabins. The poles were then securely fastened together with hickory bark, woven in and out between the poles, making a stockade seven to eight feet high. This frail protection afforded the men some little security against prowling bears and Native Americans. They only lived here a short time before Native American attacks threatened the surveyors and settlers. Lord Dunmore, governor of Virginia, would later send Daniel Boone and Michael Stoner to recall the surveyors and empty out Kentucky.[91]

Within two weeks, Isaac Hite and his band of eleven men joined Harrod at Harrod's Town. Most of these men had fought in the French and Indian

Wars. Rendezvousing near the Big Spring, east of town, the men proceeded with great eagerness to locate and select by lot places suitable for building cabins. They also founded and claimed Fountainbleu Spring. The men of Hite's company "improved" the site, generally without building cabins, but the Big Spring was the rallying point for both groups of settlers. The first corn crop in Kentucky was planted in Harrodsburg by John Harmon and at Fountainbleu by David Williams, John Shelp and James Sodowski in 1774.[92]

Harrod's group had cleared out of Harrodsburg by the end of July 1774, before Boone and Stoner arrived. James Harrod's militia marched on to Point Pleasant to fight in Lord Dunmore's War, but they arrived too late to participate in the fighting. The conflict resulted from escalating violence between white settlers who were exploring and moving into land south of the Ohio River (modern West Virginia, southwestern Pennsylvania and Kentucky) and Native Americans, who had rights to hunt there. Incursions and successive attacks by settlers on Indian lands provoked war bands to retaliate. War was declared "to pacify the hostile Indian war bands." The war ended soon after Virginia's victory in the Battle of Point Pleasant on October 10, 1774.

On March 8, 1775, Harrod led a group of forty or more men back to Harrod's Town to stay at the first permanent settlement in Kentucky. Flooding had ruined many of the structures built the previous summer, and the land was soaked, so these cabins were abandoned; the decision was made to construct a log fort on the hill west of the Big Spring. The site of the fort, to be started later in the summer, was chosen by Harrod because it had several good springs and good view of the town site and the adjoining countryside.[93]

Harrod's Town had lush grass and abundant water, and the limestone soil made it a pastureland for grass-eating animals that was without parallel in pioneer history. Bears provided an excellent meat substitute for bacon. Game was plentiful, but so were Indian raids. The new fort was nearly completed and conveniently located; it provided refuge for both the people of Harrod's Town and other settlers when the Native Americans were on the warpath. The fort of 1775–76 was located about one-half mile south of the Big Spring and was built on higher ground than the 1774 Big Spring's encampment. The higher ground allowed an unobstructed view in all directions. There were numerous springs at the newer site, with a natural spring being located within the walls of the fort. This spring was a primary water source for the people of the fort and always supplied them with a constant water supply.[94]

At this time in history, the overflow from the Big Spring formed two small streams: the present channel known as the Town Creek and another branch from the Gore Spring. By 1806, Ann McGinty had the first fulling mill in

Harrodsburg, located on the Gore Spring. In many places, traces of the bed of this stream can still be found, but the water has long since ceased to flow. As the town built up, people began to dig wells and tap the underground streams. This reduced the volume of water in the Big Spring, and the cutting away of the heavy timber to build the fort and town allowed more chance for evaporation from the sun's rays, so in time the shallower channel dried up. The Gore Spring was eventually filled in and paved over, leaving the Big Spring as the major water supply to the Town Creek.

During pioneer times, hardly a week went by without one or more deaths because of ordinary activities near the fort. On June 22, 1777, one man, Barney Stagner, carelessly wandered outside the fort above the Big Spring, against Harrod's orders. He was killed and scalped by the Native Americans. They cut off his head and stuck it on a pole. For years after that, people living near the fort used to say that at night when the moon was full, they could see a ghost around the fort springs.[95]

Today, the area around the Big Spring has been turned into a small walking park. Big Spring Park allows for leisurely walks around the historic spring and picnics near the water.

Gore Springs

Located at the northwest corner of the original Old Fort Harrod, the "old fort spring" or original "town spring" has been for many years entirely dry and paved over. The veins that supplied it so abundantly when it was first discovered and became historic 250 years ago seem all to have been stopped up or diverted into the Big Spring, forming the present Town Creek. Historians have referenced this water as the Gore Springs, after Andrew Gore, who purchased the spring from the heirs of William Pogue, second husband of Ann McGinty, in about 1815. Early Harrodsburg maps show Gore Springs located 265 feet west of the old spring at the northwest corner of the original Fort Harrod.[96]

The most notable accomplishment related to Gore Springs, besides supplying Fort Harrod, was the establishment of Ann McGinty's fulling mill. A fulling mill was used to break down fibers like nettles and hemp and cleanse, shrink and thicken the cloth. McGinty is known for producing linsey-woolsey, a fiber made from native nettles and buffalo hair. In early 1800s, as the stream of immigration was increasing, many home seekers and land speculators came to Harrodsburg, and there was in demand

A historical postcard of Old Fort Harrod Spring at Pioneer Memorial Park. *Author's collection.*

for boardinghouses and taverns. Ann Pogue, so thrifty and industrious within the fort, was one of the first to secure a license to run an ordinary (boardinghouse) in 1786.

McGinty has been called the first home economics teacher of Kentucky because she brought the first spinning wheel west of the Allegheny Mountains. She was a hardy woman, considering the young mortality of the pioneer years, and she outlived four husbands. Her most famous husband (the second) and the father of her children was William Pogue. He became the woodworker at Fort Harrod, building the first weaving loom in Kentucky. When William died in 1781 near Fort Logan, Ann quickly married Joseph Lindsay because she was a widow with young children. Unfortunately, less than a year into this marriage, Lindsay became the first victim at the Battle of Blue Licks in August 1782. After his death, Ann waited until 1785 before she married James McGinty.

The license for her fulling mill on Gore Springs was issued in the name of Ann Lindsay, so it must have been established in 1781, although the first mention of this mill was 1803. In 1786, her ordinary was licensed under the name Ann McGinty, but in 1788, the license was granted to her and her husband. Records also mention McGinty's fulling mill near Gore's spring in 1805, the same year a Harrodsburg committee was appointed by the trustees to examine the streets adjacent to her mill. There is no mention of the McGinty Fulling Mill after 1806.

Boiling Springs

James Harrod was the founder of the second-oldest settlement in Kentucky, known then as Boiling Springs, now in present-day Danville. When Harrodsburg was founded in 1774, the pioneers had a lottery for in-lots and out-lots throughout the area. James Harrod drew an out-lot at Boiling Spring, about five miles east of Harrodsburg. He proceeded to build a number of rude log cabins. Harrod built at Boiling Spring because he was guaranteed a bountiful, flowing supply of fresh water. Historians have also referred to another spring, Payne's Spring, located near Boiling Spring.[97]

With challenges from the Transylvania Company, Harrod stated that his men had arrived first to Kentucky and had started a town. The men marking land were working for those who had returned to the settlement in order to bring out more supplies or their families. Everyone wanted good land, and Kentucky was a new country with plenty of land for all.[98]

On May 7, 1775, Harrod and Colonel Thomas Slaughter came to Boonesborough to ask Richard Henderson, head of the Transylvania Company, to settle the land dispute. While Harrod and Slaughter argued, Colonel Henderson saw himself as an uneasy mediator. Henderson secretly favored Slaughter, but fearing Harrod's wrath, he refrained from voicing this conviction and tried to appear impartial. Henderson proposed that the different settlements in Kentucky should send delegates to Boonesborough on May 23 and form a representative government to make laws and rules to prevent trouble. The four distinct settlements—Boonesborough, Harrod's Town, Boiling Spring Station and Logan's Station (formerly St. Asaph)—agreed to meet at Boonesborough to draw up a constitution and make laws.[99]

As the host settlement, Boonesborough was allowed six delegates, and Harrod's Town, Boiling Springs and Logan's Station were allowed four delegates each. Henderson explained the rights of the assembly, its policies for the colony and the procedures that were to be followed. The assembly would remain in jurisdiction of the territory, and land would be sold at company prices. The eighteen elected delegates would make up the lower house of a legislature, but the owners would constitute the upper house. Henderson would provide executive leadership, and the assembly would collect feudal-type land taxes of two shillings per hundred acres. English common law dealing with landownership was based on the feudal system, in which the monarch owned all the land but allowed favored individuals the use of it as tenants.[100]

Kentucky was fast becoming a white man's land. Henderson had already opened a land office at Boonesborough and was granting land to actual settlers. He had also made out commissions for local officers at Logan's Station, Boiling Springs and Harrod's Town. He had taken occasion to personally visit the three forts and found with a degree of pleasure that although provisions, especially salt, were scarce, the people seemed prosperous and well pleased with Kentucky and the Transylvania Company.[101]

When Henderson had opened the earlier convention, he bowed to the attentiveness of Virginia's royal governor, but he then went calmly on with his own undertakings. However, some of the settlers were having problems with Henderson's decisions, especially over at Harrod's Town and Boiling Springs, where Captain Harrod's influence was prevailing, and disillusionment began to appear. Harrod had been hoping to secure political privileges and large tracts of land for himself, and his friends had induced his supporters to send a letter of protest.[102]

By the time of Harrod's marriage in February 1778 to Ann Coburn McDaniel, his new station at Boiling Springs was incomplete and too isolated for safety, so he took Ann straight on to Fort Harrod, where they lived until the next fall. Although no exact description exists of Boiling Springs, it is said to have been several cabins surrounded by a stockade. Living there were the families James Coburn (Ann's brother), Henry Prathers and Isaac Pritchards; Samuel and Margaret Coburn (Ann Harrod's parents); and Jacob Kelly and several of Harrod's nephews, one of them also named James.

Harrod's Station at Boiling Springs was fortified in 1779, and James built Ann a large twin-chimney frame house on the property. This was the first house of its kind in Kentucky; unfortunately, it was destroyed by arson in 1833. At this site alone, Harrod had a total of 2,818 acres in what is now Mercer and Boyle Counties. He had numerous other landholdings in Kentucky, particularly along the Green River south of his settlement. Because of the spaciousness of their home, the hospitality of Ann and the somewhat safe location, their house became a preaching place and stopover for early Methodist itinerant preachers.

Boiling Springs continued to grow and flourished, and the fortification was never successfully breached by Indian attacks. The station also housed the influx of the Low Dutch, whom Harrod allowed to build cabins, clear and farmland until they could fortify their own claims. The Old Dutch Station was established nearby on Harrod land.

At this time in history, commissioners used well-known spots as the basis for determination of boundaries—Harrod's Landing, Harrod's Fort,

Chaplin's Fork, Harrod's Creek, Boiling Springs and so on—and Harrod testified frequently during sessions of land court, especially for members of his family. For his stepson, "James Harrod this day appeared and claimed a right to a settlement and preemption as guardian to James McDaniel." This was referring to land on Gilbert's Creek, settled 1776 by the boy's late father. On his own behalf, Harrod claimed settlement and preemption to a tract of land lying on Harrod's Run now known as Boiling Spring, because of the improvements made in 1774, 1775 and 1776.[103]

Harrod was happiest when he had children around him. His nephews Thomas, William Harrod Jr. and James Harrod, his namesake, had been living at Boiling Springs for several years. Since the death of John Harrod Jr. (James's half brother) a few days after Christmas 1781, his wife had been sending messages trying to get Harrod to bring twenty-year-old Thomas back to Bedford so he could look after her and his sisters. So, while Ann Harrod was visiting with her family in North Carolina, her husband used the time to return Thomas mother.

Upon his return to Kentucky, Harrod turned his thoughts to the establishment of the new district court and his seat on the grand jury. He heard cases on the selling of spirituous liquors without a license, adultery, fornication and the irregularity on the part of the Lincoln county clerk. The first court met at Harrodsburg, but because there was no adequate building, the justices authorized a new one to be built. The court was temporarily at Crow's station, not far from Boiling Springs, near the Town Spring in present-day Danville. The new building was large enough to have a courtroom at one end and two jury rooms on the other. They also built a jail of hewed, sawed logs at least nine inches thick.[104]

Boiling Springs Station had become a regular stopping place for Virginia land speculators, and Harrod wanted to provide a few refinements. His house had simple furnishings but included more than a dozen books and a few pieces of queen's ware and Delftware, a blue-and-white pottery made in and around Delft in the Netherlands. James no longer had to go to Fort Pitt to buy rifles and accessories because good gunsmiths were setting up business in Harrodsburg and Louisville.[105]

John Fauntleroy was an eight-year-old student at Harrod's Latin School from 1786 to 1787, but after the school was closed, he finished his education in Lexington; he would later return to marry Margaret Harrod, James's only natural-born child. Margaret died on August 25, 1841, at Boiling Springs at the age of nearly fifty-six years, leaving a large number of worthy descendants. Ann Harrod lived to be eighty-eight years old and died at Boiling Springs on April 14, 1843. She was among the very last of the distinguished pioneer women of Kentucky.

The Methodist church held its first quarterly conference at Boiling Springs in 1786. According to Ann Harrod, sixty-five "worshippers gathered around the hearth," and many passionate services were held. There were many converts, and Ann "became a devout and influential member of the Methodist congregation."[106]

Harrod wanted a large landed estate for his heirs, which were only Ann and Margaret after the death of his stepson in 1787. Possessing large acres was a symbol of pride to Harrod, and he owned a large amount of land: 1,300 acres at Boiling Springs, 1,400 acres in Lincoln County, 18,000 acres in Jefferson County and 700 acres in Mercer County. He also surveyed 200,000 to 300,000 acres in the Green River country, but he lost most of this due to inadequate paperwork.[107]

When Harrod was at Boiling Springs, he enjoyed his new house. All around it was rich land filled with crops, and slaves worked the fields. He cherished his feather beds, which were filled with the feathers from the geese on the farm. He also had twenty-eight sheep to provide wool for clothing and twenty milk cows and eighteen hogs for food. They also had plates and chair enough for a dozen guests at meals.[108]

Fountainbleu

Fountainbleu (or Fountain Blue or Fountain Bleau) was a large spring three miles below where the original Harrod's company landed and was founded by Isaac Hite and his party of eleven men, who joined the Harrod party on June 27, 1774. The first corn in Kentucky was planted at the original Harrod's Town site by John Harmon and at Fountainbleu by David Williams, John Shelp and James Sodowski in 1774.[109]

However, nineteen days later, on July 16, 1774, James Harrod's dream of a permanent settlement in Kentucky abruptly came to an end. Nine men from Harrod's Town were busy at their favorite task of claiming and surveying land and were camped at Fountainbleu Springs. Suddenly, they were attacked by twenty Shawnee warriors, who instantly killed James Cowan and James Hamilton. Two Native Americans closely chased George Pogue, a nephew of Colonel William Pogue—he did not even have time to turn and shoot. They were so close that they tried to seize his gun, which he threw to one side. The Native Americans grabbed the gun and fired at

Pogue with his own gun but missed. He escaped to Harrod's Town along with the other survivors and reported the tragedy to their leader. Captain Harrod collected the other men in the neighborhood, thirty-five in number, and returned to the site of the battle, but the Indians had disappeared.[110]

During the same period as Harrod's arrival in Kentucky, Colonel William Preston, the official surveyor of Fincastle County, sent three deputy surveyors to the west: Hancock Taylor, James Douglas and John Floyd. The Fincastle surveyors were working on the east side of the Kentucky River when they first learned of the attack at Fountainbleu Springs. They successfully fled from the country after leaving a note on a tree for their uninformed companions. Floyd and his three men wandered into Harrodsburg, where they found the note and returned home safely. Hancock Taylor and one of his assistants, James Strother, were not so fortunate. Like Hamilton and Cowan, they became victims of the Shawnees as well.[111]

According to historians, Fountainbleu got its name from the small lake near the center of the property that at one point appeared to have bright-blue water. The first records of actual horse racing in Kentucky were the 1783 competitions at Harrodsburg's "Humble's race path" near Fountainbleu in April. Moving into the next century, Fountainbleu was owned for many years by the Forsythe family.

The first representative of the Forsythe family in Kentucky was Matthew Forsythe, who was born in South Carolina on March 5, 1769. He came to Kentucky with Governor Adair just after the surrender of Cornwallis at Yorktown in 1781 and settled on the Fountainbleu Springs farm. He served four years in the War of 1812, took part in several expeditions against the Native Americans and afterward devoted his time to farming and stock raising at Fountainbleu.

In about 1790, Forsythe married Jane McAfee, daughter of Robert McAfee, and their son was Robert McAfee Forsythe. Robert was also a soldier in the War of 1812 and afterward retired to farm life and became a well-known farmer and horse breeder. He also had a son named Robert, who would become the father of James M. Forsythe Sr. James was born on January 18, 1809, at Fountainbleu, and the farm then consisted of 460 acres of good "bottom" land near Salt River.

Boise House was built at Fountainbleu Springs in 1817. It was listed in the National Register of Historic Places in 1989. This Federal-style home was a one-and-a-half-story brick and block house laid in Flemish bond with five bays, flanked on either side by two-bay wings. The floor plan of the main structure had a central hall, two rooms deep, with arched exterior doors into

A photograph of Fountainbleu, or Boise House, located on Fountainbleu Springs. *Clay Lancaster.*

the central hall. The brick chimneys were placed on the interior at the gable ends, and the foundation was dry-laid stone. All the interior woodwork was attributed to Matthew Lowery, and it retained a beaded chair rail, six-panel doors and rosettes in the door frames and some of the mantels. A one-room brick addition was built onto the northeast wing.

Howard Forsythe, son of James Forsythe, was born on Fountainbleu farm on August 29, 1864. As an adult, he bred a special type of racehorse, but later in life he devoted most of his time to saddle-horses and Thoroughbreds Soon his time and attention were given over to farming and to the raising of horses, cattle and hogs.

A photograph of Fountainbleu. This home has been demolished. *Jerry L. Sampson.*

Fountainbleu is famous for producing two Kentucky Derby winners. Leonatus, winner of the ninth Kentucky Derby (1883), was noted for his stamina and durability. He was owned by George Morgan and Colonel Jack P. Chinn, both of Mercer County. Leonatus was foaled in 1880 on Fountainbleu Springs, and he died in 1898 in Bourbon County. As a two-year-old, Leonatus only ran one race, in which he came in second, but as a three-year-old, he put together an amazing string of victories. Leonatus was trained by African American horseman Raleigh Colston Sr., as well as by John McGinty.

An interesting tidbit about the Kentucky Derby surfaced during research about Fountainbleu. According to legend, in 1883 Harrodsburg native Jack Chinn and another horse owner placed a bet of roses on the winning horse. Leonatus distinguished himself by eating the presentation roses. Blankets of roses were not recorded as being draped over the winning Derby horse until 1896, when Ben Brush was the winning horse.

In 1916, Harrodsburg had another Kentucky Derby winner. George Smith was a black colt named after noted turfman George E. Smith, also known as "Pittsburg Phill," who was once an owner of the colt's dam. The horse was bred by Fred Forsythe and Jack Chinn and was foaled at their Fountainbleu Springs Farm. George Smith was purchased as a yearling for $1,600 by Ed McBride, who trained him as a yearling and raced him as a two-year-old before he went on to win the Kentucky Derby.

By the turn of the twenty-first century, a small footprint of the original Fountainbleu Springs remained, but most of the land has been subdivided for homes. The site of the historic spring is on private property.

Shawnee Springs

Shawnee Springs is known historically as the Hugh McGary Station. McGary was a member of Harrodsburg's founding party and was known as a bit of a hothead. He was the stepfather of James Ray, who would grow to be another great leader from Harrodsburg. When Harrod's party returned to Kentucky in 1775, Major McGary took up a large land grant north of Fort Harrod, his acres extending from Shawnee Springs to what is now the Louisville Pike.

Historians tell the story of a sixteen-year-old James Ray helping to clear the lands at Shawnee Springs, killing a wild duck at the springs and cooking it over a bonfire. A stranger on horseback rode up as he prepared to enjoy his feast, and the young man invited him to share the duck. The Kentucky hospitality of this pioneer to a hungry stranger was important because that stranger was George Rogers Clark, on his way from Virginia to Fort Harrod in the fall of 1775.

The most dramatic episode connected with Shawnee Springs was the attack of Native Americans led by Chief Blackfish on four settlers cutting trees around the springs: James and William Ray, William Coomes and Thomas Shores. James Ray fled from the scene and ran the six miles or more back to Fort Harrod to warn the settlers. William Ray, his younger brother, and Shores were killed, but Coomes, concealed in the thick foliage of a tree that had just been cut, escaped detection and was later rescued by the fort dwellers. James Ray, as he grew older, became one of the most beloved, helpful and constructive men of the pioneer settlement and was commissioned a general in the frontier army. He must have inherited some of his stepfather's land, for he lived and died at Shawnee Springs and was buried in a family graveyard there. He died in 1830, and his grave was set along Shawnee Springs under an apple tree at his own request. When a photograph was taken of the grave, only a stump of the apple tree

This is the grave of James Ray. His remains were removed from Shawnee Springs and reinterred at the Pioneer Cemetery at Old Fort Harrod State Park. *Keith Rightmyer.*

remained. His body was later exhumed and reburied at the Pioneer Cemetery at Old Fort Harrod State Park. General Ray served in the Kentucky legislature for the years 1801–3, 1809–11, 1814–15 and 1818. His grave is marked only by the stump of the old tree. It is probable that the body will be exhumed and buried at the city cemetery. Ray lived in a commodious double log cabin in front of whose doors a great elm spread its branches, and when he died, hundreds of people from distant places came to attend his funeral. The crowd was so large that the services were held under the shade of this tree in order that all might hear the funeral sermon.[112]

Mr. and Mrs. Henry Cleveland Wood, two loyal friends of Fort Harrod, made an interesting and valuable donation to the fort. The gift is the framed initials of Daniel Boone, which has been displayed at both the Chicago and St. Louis Expositions. Collins's *History of Kentucky* tells us that Daniel Boone spent the winter of 1769–70 in a cave near the waters of Shawnee Springs in Mercer County. A tree with his initials was growing near the head of the cave. For many years, these initials were protected by a glass frame fastened on the side of the tree, while above the frame was nailed a pair of antlers. The letters were later cut from the tree and present to the Woods by the current owner of the farm. The name of Boone is a magic one, and this gift from Mr. and Mrs. Wood is looked on with great interest by visitors of Fort Harrod.[113]

The Shawnee Springs home was a Flemish-bond brick house, built between 1788 and 1792, and is thought to be one of the earliest houses built in Mercer County. It is listed in the National Register of Historic Places, one of the first in the county to be put on the register. By being in the register, Shawnee Springs' owner becomes eligible for federal grants-in-aid for historic preservation through state programs. The original Shawnee Springs home burned to the ground in 1801. It was rebuilt in 1805 with seventeen staircases to enable its occupants to escape easily from future fires.[114]

This house was built by George Thompson, one of the early settlers from Virginia. The Thompson family occupied the house for four generations,

A historical postcard of Boone's Cave, where Daniel Boone spent the winter of 1769–70. *Author's collection.*

The piece of the tree from outside the Daniel Boone cave, where Boone carved his initials. This is preserved under glass at the Mansion Museum at Old Fort Harrod State Park. *Old Fort Harrod State Park.*

A historic postcard of a Shawnee Springs house, the George C. Thompson House. *Author's collection.*

and his great-grandchildren were born in the house. Built at the head of Shawnee Springs, the house featured a center section with wings. The front hallway ran the entire width of the house. Four large columns, made of brick and covered with plaster, were at the front of the house. Native woods were used throughout the house: the fluted columns were made of poplar and ash and the stairs were made of cherry.[115]

An especially honored guest, Marie-Joseph Paul Yves Gilbert du Motier, the Marquis de Lafayette, the last surviving French general of the Revolutionary War, arrived at Shawnee Springs on May 16, 1825. There is a photostatic copy of Lafayette's speech at Transylvania University in the handwriting of his son, George Washington Lafayette, and another of the letter written by Henry Clay in Washington on January 15, 1825, to his friend, Major George Thompson, who had been aide-de-camp for Lafayette during the Revolution and was the current resident at Shawnee Springs, regarding plans for entertaining the French general.[116]

The 134th anniversary of the founding of Harrodsburg, the oldest city in Kentucky, was celebrated at Shawnee Springs on June 16, 1908. An old-fashioned basket dinner was prepared. The Harrodsburg Historical Society completed all arrangements for the celebration, and several distinguished historians outside of Mercer County were invited to participate. The program for this celebration included:

Opening Address—Col. J. Stoddard Johnston
The Cradle of the Commonwealth—Mrs. W.L. Beardsley
Notable Men of Shawnee Run—Hon. W.W. Stephenson
Old Graham Springs—Mr. Henry Cleveland Wood
Romances of Early Harrodsburg—Miss Neva L. Williams
The Press of Harrodsburg—Mr. Lew B. Brown
The Pioneer Child's Education—Miss Martha Stephenson
The Future Harrodsburg—Mr. N.L. Curry[117]

In the 1960s, the current owners were suffering from ill health and moved closer to town. They leased Shawnee Springs to be used as a restaurant and boardinghouse. This became the home of Renfrew House, a restaurant operated by Robert Renfrew. Before this time, Renfrew was the owner of the Trustee's Office at Shaker Village of Pleasant Hill and turned it into a restaurant in the late 1950s. While the Renfrew House was in operation, it was the premier Harrodsburg destination for engagement parties, weddings, birthdays and other celebrations.

In August 1982, the Shawnee Springs Farmhouse was in the process of being remodeled when it was gutted by fire. An estimated one-half to two-thirds of the Greek Revival house on Curry Lane was burned when a fire swept through the home. The present owner was in the process of remodeling the nearly two-hundred-year-old structure. The cause of the fire was investigated, but the fire is thought to have started in the attic due to the

A photograph of the Renfro House and the Farmstead at Shawnee Springs. *Farmstead at Shawnee Springs.*

electrical wiring. At the scene, firefighters were busy trying to save the west wing of the house, as the central portion was completely destroyed.

Under the current owners, the home was rebuilt, and Farmstead at Shawnee Springs currently offers wedding packages for planning your perfect celebration. The barn is 105 years old; the wood and warm runway lighting are original. The venue has more than 1,100 square feet of climate-controlled rooms for comfort during the day before your party starts.

Cove Spring

Corn was planted and raised at Cove Spring, and according to Collins's *History of Kentucky*, William Pogue, second wife of Ann McGinty, cleared ground and raised corn here in 1776. This spring was the site of a conflict that became legendary to the locals of the area.

The "corn crib skirmish" of Harrodsburg occurred on September 22, 1777, but started two weeks earlier. A party of thirty-seven men under Colonel Bowman went to Captain Joseph Bowman's settlement at the Cove Spring, five miles southeast of Harrodsburg, to shell corn and bring it back to the fort. The "skirmish" occurred when a party of Kickapoos crept through a canebrake and fired at the pioneers as they were shelling corn. Bowman gallantly yelled to his men, "Stand your ground!—we are able to beat them, by the Lord!" Squire Boone and James Berry, along with five others, were injured, with one dying later that night. Eli Gerrard was killed instantly, but Nathaniel Randolph ran all the way to Harrodsburg to get help. This spirited little affair was also known among the frontiersmen of the day as the "Battle of Cove Spring."

NOTES

Introduction

1. Cummings, *Sketches of a Tour to the Western Country*, 7.

Chapter 1

2. Mercer County Court Deed Book 9, 37.
3. Van Arsdall, "Springs at Harrodsburg," 309.
4. Ibid., 308.
5. Ibid., 309; Circuit Court Records, Mercer County, Box J 5–9, Packet 7, and Box E 5, Packet 5.
6. Van Arsdall, "Springs at Harrodsburg," 310.
7. Ibid., 311.
8. *Kentucky Gazette*, August 25, 1812.
9. Van Arsdall, "Springs at Harrodsburg," 312.
10. Ibid., 313.
11. Mercer County Records Order Book, 1793–1801, 101.
12. Coleman, "Old Kentucky Watering Places," 20; *Kentucky Gazette*, May 23, 1809.
13. Smith, *Complete Index to…Littell's Laws of Kentucky*, 55.
14. Van Arsdall, "Springs at Harrodsburg," 313–14.
15. *Register of the Kentucky Historical Society*, 1963, 311.

16. Van Arsdall, *Medical History of the Harrodsburg Springs*.
17. *Kentucky Gazette*, August 25, 1812.
18. Mercer County Court Deed Book 9, 37. Note: This deed was not recorded until March 10, 1814, when Head sold the lot to Eleanor Kincaid.
19. Mercer County Deed Book 7, 219.
20. A ropewalk, or a factory for making hemp rope and bagging, was an accepted and easy way to make "quick money." The Deep South was anxious for the bagging to use around cotton bales, and this section of Kentucky grew much hemp.
21. Circuit Court Records, Judgements, Box B, Packet 54, 1827; Mercer Circuit Court Records, *Bibb-Eastland v. Van Arsdel*, 274–78.
22. *Kentucky Gazette*, March 11, 1816; *Kentucky Gazette*, August 25, 1812; Van Arsdall, "Springs at Harrodsburg," 319–20.
23. Mercer County Deed Book 9, 164–241; Mercer County Records Plat Book I, 75.
24. *Olive Branch and Western Union*, June 16, 1820.
25. Ludlow, *Dramatic Life as I Found It*, 91–93.
26. Mercer County Deed Book 9, 229; Deed Book 11, 72; Deed Book 11, 63.
27. The main outlet for Harrodsburg Springs—sometimes called "Saloon Springs"—is now in Young's Park near the James B. Haggin Memorial Hospital.
28. Mercer County Deed Book 12, 168; Deed Book 11, 391; *Olive Branch and Western Union*, May 19, 1820; Mercer County Circuit Court, Judgements, Box H, Packet 75.
29. Mercer County Deed Book 11, 348–416; Deed Book 12, 47–425.
30. Mercer County Deed Book 13, 368–76; Van Arsdall, *Medical History of the Harrodsburg Springs*, 389.
31. Mercer County Deed Book 16, 253.
32. Mercer County Deed Book 18, 525.
33. Stephenson, "Education in Harrodsburg and Neighborhood since 1775," 31–42.
34. *Courier-Journal*, June 19, 1845.
35. *College of the Bible Quarterly*, 20; Mercer County Deed Book 18, 525; Deed Book 26, 130–562; *Harrodsburg Herald*, March 27, 1922.
36. *Courier-Journal*, July 23, 1851.
37. *Acts of the General Assembly of the Commonwealth of Kentucky, Passed*, 114.
38. Daughters College, *Daughters College*, 20–21.
39. Ibid., 22.

40. Williams, "Educational Announcement of Daughters' College," *Register of the Kentucky Historical Society* (1963), quoted in Bourne, *History of Daughters College*, 9–11.

Chapter 2

41. Bryant, *Christopher Columbus Graham*, 2–3.
42. Stephenson, "Old Graham Springs," 30.
43. Bryant, *Christopher Columbus Graham*, 3.
44. *Courier-Journal*, June 25, 1841.
45. Clark, *Kentucky*, 239.
46. Stephenson, "Old Graham Springs," 27–35.
47. *Courier-Journal*, November 17, 1929.
48. Ibid.
49. Clark, *Kentucky*, 223.
50. Ibid.
51. Ibid.
52. United States Supreme Court, *Strader v. Graham*, 51 U.S. 82, 1851.
53. Ibid.
54. Ibid.
55. Ibid.
56. Ibid.
57. Ibid.
58. Ibid.
59. Matthews, "Old Mystery Is Cleared Up."
60. *Lexington Herald*, July 23, 1932.

Chapter 3

61. *Register of the Kentucky Historical Society*, vols. 11–12, 35.
62. Armstrong, *Harrodsburg and Mercer County*, 82.
63. MacGowan, *The Tradesman*, 47:34.
64. *Kentucky Advocate*, 1911.
65. *Kentucky Advocate*, February 26, 1920; *Harrodsburg Democrat*, December 18, 1919.
66. *Richmond Daily Register*, August 17, 1920.
67. *Advocate-Messenger*, November 4, 1920.

68. *Lexington Leader*, June 17, 1923.
69. *Advocate-Messenger*, June 16, 1923.
70. *Advocate-Messenger*, August 8, 1924.
71. *Advocate-Messenger*, June 11, 1926.
72. *Lexington Herald*, June 19, 1927.
73. *Interior Journal*, July 6, 1928; *Courier-Journal*, August 5, 1928.
74. *Advocate-Messenger*, March 15, 1929.
75. *Kentucky Advocate*, September 14, 1932.
76. *Advocate-Messenger*, May 13, 1933.
77. *Advocate-Messenger*, May 2, 1935.
78. *Lexington Herald*, June 14, 1937.
79. *Advocate-Messenger*, August 5, 1938.
80. *Lexington Herald*, July 27, 1939.
81. *Lexington Herald*, July 7, 1941.
82. *Lexington Leader*, October 26, 1945.
83. *Courier-Journal*, November 25, 1945.
84. *Lexington Herald*, December 2, 1945.
85. *Lexington Herald*, April 2, 1946.
86. *Lexington Leader*, April 20, 1947.
87. *Advocate Messenger*, July 21, 1948.
88. *Lexington Leader*, December 13, 1953.

Chapter 4

89. Collins and Collins, *History of Kentucky*, 517; Harrison, *New History of Kentucky*, chapter 3; "A Sketch of Captain (Abraham) Chapline," Draper Collection, MS 4cc33.
90. Kleber, *Kentucky Encyclopedia*, 414.
91. *Harrodsburg Herald*, January 12, 1995.
92. Clark, *Voice of the Frontier*, 10; Collins and Collins, *History of Kentucky*, 517; Beckner, "Captain James Harrod's Company," 282.
93. Collins and Collins, *History of Kentucky*, 518–19; Harrison, *New History of Kentucky*, 24–25.
94. Kleber, *Kentucky Encyclopedia*, 344.
95. Draper Collection, 26cc55, 4cc30.
96. *Lexington Leader*, June 25, 1922.
97. Clark, *History of Kentucky*, 13, 36.
98. Collins, *Historical Sketches of Kentucky*, 499–500.

99. Cotterill, *History of Pioneer Kentucky*, Kindle, 1,460–83.
100. Harrison, *New History of Kentucky*, 29.
101. Cotterill, *History of Pioneer Kentucky*, Kindle, 1,552–63.
102. Caruso, *Appalachian Frontier*, Kindle, 2,795–96.
103. *Register of the Kentucky Historical Society*, vols. 5–7.
104. Stephenson, "Old Courthouse and the Courts and Bar of Mercer County."
105. Dillin, *Kentucky Rifle*, 13.
106. Draper Collection, 12cc25.
107. Jillson, "Old Kentucky Entries and Deeds," 38, 217, 419, 498, 562.
108. Klotter, *History Mysteries*, 24.
109. Clark, *Voice of the Frontier*, 10.
110. Force, *American Archives*, 1:707–8; O'Malley, *Boonesborough Unearthed*, 223–37.
111. Belue, *Hunters of Kentucky*, 73; Kleber, *Encyclopedia of Louisville*, 499; Brown, *Frontiersman*; Tillson, *Gentry and Common Folk*, 22–25.
112. *Courier-Journal*, June 17, 1908.
113. *Kentucky Advocate*, February 8, 1929.
114. *Advocate-Messenger*, July 29, 1976.
115. *Advocate-Messenger*, August 22, 1982.
116. *Lexington Leader*, May 20, 1934.
117. *Lexington Leader*, June 12, 1908.

BIBLIOGRAPHY

Acts of the General Assembly of the Commonwealth of Kentucky, Passed. Vol. 2. *Kentucky Law Review* (1851).

Advocate-Messenger. Danville, Kentucky.

Armstrong, Anna. *Harrodsburg and Mercer County*. Charleston, SC: Arcadia Publishing, 2013.

Armstrong, Anna, and Bobbi Rightmyer. *Harrodsburg*. Images of America series. Charleston, SC: Arcadia Publishing, 2011.

Beckner, Lucien. "Captain James Harrod's Company." *Register of Kentucky State Historical Society* 20, no. 60 (September 1922).

Belue, Ted Franklin. *The Hunters of Kentucky: A Narrative History of America's First Far West, 1750–1790*. Mechanicsburg, PA: Stackpole Books, 2011.

Bourne, Anne Shanks. *History of Daughters College, 1856–1893, and Its Founder, John Augustus Williams*. Harrodsburg, KY: Hutton Publishing, 1907.

Brown, Meredith M. *Frontiersman: Daniel Boone and the Making of America*. Baton Rouge: Louisiana State University Press, 2008.

Brown, Richard C. "Graham Expanded Springs' Resort." *Advocate-Messenger*, September 22, 2002.

Bryant, Ron. *Christopher Columbus Graham: An Extraordinary Kentuckian*. Frankfort: SOS of KY, 2006.

Caruso, Dr. John A. *The Appalachian Frontier: America's First Surge Westward*. Knoxville: University of Tennessee Press, 2017.

Clark, Thomas D. *A History of Kentucky*. Lexington: University Press of Kentucky, 1950.

———. *The Kentucky*. Lexington: University Press of Kentucky, Lexington, 2021.

Clark, Thomas D., ed. *The Voice of the Frontier: John Bradford's Notes on Kentucky*. Lexington: University Press of Kentucky, 1993.

Coleman, J. Winston. "Old Kentucky Watering Places." *Filson Club History Quarterly* 16 (1942).

College of the Bible Quarterly 29 (1962).

Collins, Lewis. *Historical Sketches of Kentucky: History of Kentucky*. Vol. 2. Lexington, KY: Collins & Company, 1882.

Collins, Lewis, and Richard Collins. *History of Kentucky*. Lexington, KY: Clearfield Company, 1998.

Cotterill, Robert Spencer. *The History of Pioneer Kentucky*. Cincinnati, OH: Heritage Books, Inc., 2012.

Courier-Journal. Louisville, Kentucky.

Cummings, Fortescue. *Sketches of a Tour to the Western Country*. Philadelphia, PA, 1810.

Daughters College. *Daughters College: A School for Higher Education of Young Ladies.* Harrodsburg, KY: self-published, 1888.

Daviess, Maria Thompson. *History of Mercer and Boyle Counties.* Harrodsburg, KY, 1924.

Dillin, John Grace Wolfe. *The Kentucky Rifle*. Washington, D.C., 1924.

Draper, Lyman Copeland. The Draper Manuscripts. Madison, Wisconsin: State Historical Society of Wisconsin. New York: Microfilming Corporation of America, 1982.

Force, Peter. *American Archives*. Vol. 1, *Containing a Documentary History of the United States of America, From the Declaration of Independence.* Washington, D.C.: M. St. Clair Clarke Publishing, 1846.

Harrison, Lowell. *A New History of Kentucky*. Lexington: University Press of Kentucky, 1997.

Harrodsburg Herald. Harrodsburg, Kentucky.

Heller, J. Roderick, III. *Democracy's Lawyer: Felix Grundy of the Old Southwest.* Baton Rouge: Louisiana State University Press, 2010.

Interior Journal. Stanford, Kentucky.

Jillson, Willard R. "Old Kentucky Entries and Deeds." *Filson Club Publication* 34 (1926).

Kentucky Advocate. Danville, Kentucky.

Kentucky Gazette. Lexington, Kentucky.

Kleber, John E. *The Encyclopedia of Louisville*. Louisville: University Press of Kentucky, 2000.

———. *The Kentucky Encyclopedia.* Lexington: University Press of Kentucky, 2015.

Klotter, James C. *History Mysteries.* Lexington: University Press of Kentucky, 1989.

Lexington (KY) Herald.

Lexington (KY) Herald-Leader.

Lexington (KY) Leader.

Louisville (KY) Daily Courier.

Ludlow, N.M. *Dramatic Life as I Found It.* St. Louis, MO: G.I. Jones and Company, 1880.

MacGowan, John E. *The Tradesman.* Vol. 47. Chicago, IL: Tradesman Publishing Company, 1902.

Matthews, Todd. "Old Mystery Is Cleared Up." *Mercer's Magazine* (September 2002).

McDowell, Audrey. *The Pursuit of Health and Happiness at the Paroquet Springs in Kentucky: 1838–1888.* Shepherdsville, KY: Filson Historical Society, 1995.

Mercer Circuit Court Records. *Bibb-Eastland v. Van Arsdel.* Judgements. Box B. Packet 54. 1827.

Mercer County Court Records. Deed Book 7, 9, 11.

Mercer County Records. Order Book 1793–1801.

———. Plat Book I.

Olive Branch and Western Union. Danville, Kentucky.

O'Malley, Nancy. *Boonesborough Unearthed: Frontier Archaeology at a Revolutionary Fort.* Lexington: University Press of Kentucky, 2019.

Register of the Kentucky Historical Society. Frankfort, Kentucky.

Reuben T. Durrett Collection. Christopher Columbus Graham Papers, 1860–1878. Hanna Holborn Gray Special Collections Research Center at University of Chicago Library.

Richmond (KY) Daily Register.

Smith, W.T. *A Complete Index to...Littell's Laws of Kentucky.* Lexington, KY: Clearfield Publishing, 1931.

Stephenson, Martha. "Education in Harrodsburg and Neighborhood since 1775." *Register of Kentucky State Historical Society* 9, no. 25 (January 1911).

———. "Old Graham Springs." *Register of Kentucky State Historical Society* 12, no. 34 (January 1914).

Stephenson, William Worth. "The Old Courthouse and the Courts and Bar of Mercer County." *Register of the Kentucky Historical Society* 7 (1909).

Tillson, Albert H. *Gentry and Common Folk.* Lexington: University Press of Kentucky, 2015.

U.S. Supreme Court. *Strader v. Graham*. 51 U.S. 82. 1851.

Van Arsdall, C.A. *A Medical History of the Harrodsburg Springs*. Osler Award Paper. Baltimore, MD: Johns Hopkins University, 1949.

Van Arsdall, Mai Flournoy Van Deren. "The Springs at Harrodsburg." *Register of the Kentucky Historical Society* 61, no. 4 (October 1963).

Willis, Nathaniel Parker. *Health Trip to the Tropics*. New York: C. Scribner, 1854.

INDEX

G

H

J

L

M

O

P

R

S

T

V

W

Y

ABOUT THE AUTHOR

Bobbi Dawn Rightmyer is a native of Harrodsburg, Kentucky, and writes books of narrative historical nonfiction. Her books include *Harrodsburg* (Images of America series), *Born and Raised* and *James Harrod: Founder of Harrodsburg*. She also writes historical articles for the *Harrodsburg Herald*, the *Advocate-Messenger*, *Kentucky Monthly* and *Kentucky Humanities*. Visit her website at harrodsburgsestercentennial.com.

Visit us at
www.historypress.com